GOD'S LITTLE FLOCK HEALED

"They will rise on wings like eagles: they will run and not get weary; they will walk and not grow weak." Isaiah 40:31

Stellah Mupanduki

AuthorHouse™
1663 Liberty Drive
Bloomington, IN 47403
www.authorhouse.com
Phone: 1-800-839-8640

© 2010 Stellah Mupanduki. All rights reserved.

No part of this book may be reproduced, stored in a retrieval system, or transmitted by any means without the written permission of the author.

First published by AuthorHouse 6/22/2010

ISBN: 978-1-4520-1986-4 (e)
ISBN: 978-1-4520-1984-0 (sc)
ISBN: 978-1-4520-1985-7 (hc)

Library of Congress Control Number: 2010908727

Printed in the United States of America
Bloomington, Indiana

This book is printed on acid-free paper.

CONTENTS

1. **I belong to God** 1
   We should have one authority in our lives. And that is God

2. **God hear my Prayer** 11
   God hear all our prayers. He answers them.

3. **Salvation comes from the Lord** 33
   There no other power that frees. Only God

4. **He cares** 45
   Jesus cares. He loves to help us when we reach out to him.

5. **Jesus, my Rock** 55
   We are strong in Christ. He is the one to lean on.

6. **It's Possible with God.** 69
   There is nothing God cannot do. Believe in him.

7. **My Lord and my Saviour** 87
   Christ came to save you. Trust in him.

8. **They will curse, but my God blesses.** 95
   God brought an end to suffering through his Son Jesus. We reverse all curses from attacking us in the name above.

9. **He has given me life.** 119
   We should rejoice for he died so that we live.

10. **Jesus, you love me** 129
    His love never ends, when we are weak, he is our strength.

11. **Jesus take control of my life** 141
    We surrender to Jesus and we are saved. He came so that we live life to the fullest.

12. **For, you have loved me!** 151
    God loved and gave us his Son for atonement.

13. **My God, lift me up** 159
    He is the only helper in times of our needs.

14. **His wonderful peace heals** 163
    We are free in Jesus, there is no suffering.

15. **My Redeemer lives** 173
    God is powerful and his strength is living in us.

16. **I love you Jesus** 183
    He is beautiful, compassionate and mighty to save

17. **You came for me!** 187
    He is the light for the world. He leads us on.

18. **You are my rest.** 195
    Jesus is everything we need in life. He is peace.

19. **Your eyes God.** 199
    God knows, he sees and takes account of everything.

20. **Hide me, faithful God** 203
    God`s word is flawless. It fulfill its purpose

21. **Hope for the hopeless.** 207
    We should never be troubled but trust in Jesus

22. **Re-Birth.** 209
    God delivers, revives, and restores. We are given new life. We are born again.

Chapter 1

I BELONG TO GOD

Isaiah 44:2

"I am the LORD who created you; from the time you were born, I have helped you. Do not be afraid; you are my servant, my chosen people whom I love."

Isaiah 40:11

He will take care of his flock like a shepherd; he will gather the lambs together and carry them in his arms; he will gently lead their mothers.

- ❖ We have a very good relationship with God as our good shepherd...the one who takes care of us, the one who comforts us and is there for us because he is gentle and loving...his heart is for us and he will never forsake us...he will never abandon us and he is forever with us.

Isaiah 40:21-26

Do you know?

Were you not told long ago?

Have you not heard how the world began?

It was made by the one who sits on his throne above the earth and beyond the sky; the people below look as tiny as ants. He stretched out the sky like a curtain, like a tent in which to live.

He brings down powerful rulers and reduces them to nothing. They are like young plants, just set out and barely rooted. When the LORD sends a wind, they dry up and blow away like straw.

To whom can the holy God be compared?

Is there anyone else like him?

Look up at the sky!

Who created the stars you see? The one who leads them out like an army, he knows how many they are and calls each one by name!

His power is so great- not one of them is ever missing!

❖ Our God is powerful and never fails because he created the whole world and everything in it. We are his creation and what he created, God knows how to nurture, he knows how to care for us, he knows how deep we are in trouble and sickness, nothing escapes God`s eyes and knowledge about our lives. Your pain, your fear, your agony and all difficulties you are facing is all seen by our Mighty God who is eager to save you for he is your saviour. You are under his care and he will not miss a single detail about you. He is saving you right now and he will be with you through this stormy situation. God will heal you completely because he knows how. Say "I am healed in the name of Jesus." Declare that you know the one who created you never fails and is able to save you!

Isaiah 42:8-9

"I alone am the LORD your God. No other God may share my glory; I will not let idols share my praise. The things I predicted have now come true. Now I will tell you of the new things even before they begin to happen"

❖ When God speaks healing in your life...he has already done it! All you need to do is praise him for the miracle. When God blesses you with his mercy and saving hands, then he gives you a complete new life...he speaks of it and it will unfold....what the devil wanted to take away God gives strength and purpose, he blesses so that you live to declare his goodness. He gives you his glory, his beauty and splendour because you are special. Suffering is a past thing...take his healing as a new beginning. It is already dawn...morning is coming, and the sun will rise, and your light will shine on you. Receive his word....God loves you, little one!

Isaiah 46:4

"I am your God and will take care of you until you are old and your hair is grey. I made you and will care for you; I will give you help and rescue you."

Psalm 9:1-2

I will praise you, LORD, with all my heart; I will tell of all the wonderful things you have done. I will sing with joy because of you. I will sing praise to you, almighty God.

- ❖ Yes... God wants to hear your little voice...sounding big in praising, thanking him and honouring him. You can do it because you are special to him and he is special to you. Yes he wants you to acknowledge his powerful healing in your life… saving you…upholding you and plucking you from the hands of the evil one…from the hands of death. God defeats death and breathes life into your body….nothing can take away your life; the world will not miss you, you are still living, you are still in it. Praise him for healing you. Say, "Thank you God Almighty! You are worthy of my praise."

Isaiah 61:9

They will be famous among nations; everyone who sees them will know that they are a people whom I have blessed.

Isaiah 46:13

"I am bringing the day of victory near- it is not far away at all. My triumph will not be delayed. I will save Jerusalem and bring honour to Israel there."

Luke 13:19-13

One Sabbath Jesus was teaching in a synagogue. A woman there had an evil spirit that had made her ill for eighteen years; she was bent over and could not straighten up at all. When Jesus saw her, he called out to her, "Woman, you are free from your illness!" He placed his hands on her, and once the she straightened herself up and praised God.

- ❖ God is full of mercy and compassion; even though you are not aware of his presence on you …he is still healing you. You do not need to beg him because he is aware of your situation…for he sees you. Be strong and confident in him and he will free you from the prison of disease and suffering, it does not matter how long you have endured the pain your miracle is here right now. Receive it and be healed in the name of Jesus.

1 John 5:19

We know that we belong to God even though the whole world is under the rule of the evil one.

Isaiah 44:24

"I am the LORD, your saviour; I am the one who created you. I am the LORD, the Creator of all things. I alone stretched

out the heavens; when I made the earth, no one helped me."

Ezekiel 37:4-9

He said, "Prophesy to the bones. Tell these dry bones to listen to the word of the Lord. Tell them that I, the Sovereign Lord, am saying to them: I am going to put breath into you and bring you back into life. I will give you sinews and muscles, and cover you with skin. I will put breath into you and bring you back into life. Then you will know that I am the Lord. `` So I prophesied as I had been told. While I was speaking, I heard a rattling noise, and the bones began to join together. While I watched, the bones were covered with sinews and muscles, and then the skin. But there was no breath in the bodies.

God said to me, "Mortal man, prophesy to the wind. Tell the wind that the Sovereign LORD commands it to come from every direction, to breathe into these dead bodies, and to bring them back to life."

So I prophesied as I had been told. Breath entered the bodies, and they came to life and stood up. There were enough of them to form an army.

- ❖ There is hope and a future for you. God will restore, revive and bring you back to life for you are his creation, his loved one. All those God saves, all those he heals, all those he rescues, will form an army of praise that will defeat the evil one. When we stand up to praise God for his goodness; our prayers and praise are joined together and become powerful. We have his breath us and we are his people.

Isaiah42:16

"I will lead my blind people by roads they have never travelled. I will turn their darkness into light and make rough country smooth before them. These are my promises and I will keep them without fail."

Isaiah 45:5-6

"I am the LORD; there is no other god. I will give you the strength you need, although you do not know me. I do this so that everyone from one end of the world to the other may know that I am the LORD and there is no other god."

Isaiah 64:8-9

But you are our Father, Lord. We are like clay, and you are like the potter, you created us, so do not be too angry with us or hold our sins against us forever. We are your people; be merciful to us.

Philippians 1:2

Grace and peace to you from God our Father and the Lord Jesus Christ.

1John 3:9-10

Whoever is a child of God does not continue to sin, for God`s very nature is in him; and because God is the Father, he cannot continue to sin. This is the clear difference between God`s children and the devil`s children: anyone who does not do what is right or does not love his brother is not God`s child.

Galatians 4:7

So then, you are no longer a slave but a son. And since you are his son, God will give you all that he has for his sons.

Isaiah 49:16

See, I have engraved you on the palms of my hands; your walls are ever before me.

Chapter 2
GOD HEAR MY PRAYER

Psalm 83:1

O God, do not keep silent; do not be still, do not be quiet!

Isaiah 38:17

Lord, I will live for you, for you alone; heal me and let me live.

Psalm 17:6-7

I pray to you, O God, because you answer me; so turn to me and listen to my words. Reveal your wonderful love and save us; at your side we are safe from our enemies.

Isaiah 49:8

"When the time comes to save you, I will show you favour and answer your cries for help. I will guard and protect you and through you make a covenant with all peoples."

- ❖ God wants you to live because he has a purpose for your life. You have a reason to live. Each one of us has a message for the glory of God in our lives. We live to proclaim and fulfil that he did not create us for futile reasons. We have goals and destinies that change the world and make it a better place and fulfil his purpose through us. God always put right what goes wrong in our lives; so we are healed.

Psalm 91: 14-16

God says, "I will save those who love me and will protect those who know me as LORD. When they call to me, I will answer them; when they are in trouble, I will be with them. I will rescue them and honour them. I will reward them with long life; I will save them."

- ❖ Your greatest gift to God is to love him for he has already loved you by giving you the gift of life...placing you into this world and under his care. Honour God with your life and worship him always as your only God and Saviour.

Isaiah58:9

When you pray, I will answer you, when you call me, I will respond.

- ❖ So then, pray continuously and seek his glory!

Zechariah 10:6

I will have compassion on them and bring them all back home. They will be as though I had never rejected them. I am the LORD their God; I will answer their prayers.

- ❖ Do not be afraid, God will make you strong again, he will rescue, he hears your voice and he will take away all discomfort and heal you. He will restore you back to safety and comfort. He is the God who; when you pass through the sea of trouble, in his power, he will strike the waves, and those troubles you are facing will all be driven out from your life.

Isaiah 49:6

The LORD said to me, "I have a greater task for you my servant. Not only will you restore to greatness the people of Israel who have survived, but I will also make you a light to the nations- so that the entire world may be saved."

- ❖ Because the Lord Jesus is in us and is our King, like him we have a divine appointment from our God. Because God is a God of all goodness, he saved us through his Son, we know our reason to live is for good and we will be fruitful. We are worthy to receive the blessing to live and do his will for us. It is special because it is a second chance to prove our worthy to him as our merciful God. God is healing you now because he needs you for his purpose in your life and you are a very special child of God.

Hebrews 4:16

Let us be brave, then, and approach God`s throne, where there is grace to help us just when we need it.

- ❖ When we have a relationship with God and we know that he is able and trust that he can save us, we will definitely receive his saving power, by accepting him as the one who can give us his mercy and heal us, we are humbling ourselves and not leaning on our own knowledge and understanding...we are surrendering to him because we feel only him can take away our hopelessness and helplessness feeling, only God can take away the betrayed feelings harbouring in us...giving in to God means you have reached a point where nothing else helps except his divine power and you know and believe in him as completely saving you...holding you in his comforting and life giving hands...God is restoring you; your every need will be completely met and fulfilled for he loves you. Receive healing from the Most High God in the name of Jesus.

Psalm 38:15

But I trust in you, O LORD; and you, O LORD my God, will answer me.

Isaiah 44:3-4

"I will give water to the thirsty land and make streams flow on the dry ground. I will pour out my power on your children and my blessing on your descendants. They will thrive like well watered grass, like willows by streams of running water."

2 Corinthians 10:4-5

The weapons we use in our fight are not the world`s weapons but God`s powerful weapons, which we use to destroy strongholds. We destroy false arguments; we pull down every proud obstacle that is raised against the knowledge of God; we take every thought captive and make it obey Christ.

- ❖ When facing dark times...when ill, when you are in deep troubles and suffering, resist the yoke of Satan by submitting to God...speak the good words of God...tell yourself that God is for me and wants me to be fine and therefore I shall and will be fine, pray and ask for his divine intervention in your circumstances, praise the lord, tell God you love him...him as your only God and saviour, sing to Jesus, his songs and listen to gospel music that praises and honour God...be drown in his presence, read the bible...the word of God is powerful, the devil will not stand it...disease will be conquered for you are forever calling God's help because you know he is a capable God and he will rescue. Remember Jesus died for you, for all our sins and he rose from the dead hence he conquered death and we have resurrected with him. Do not let anything tell you that there is no hope and that you are dying, declare that your life is continuing in Jesus' name and his blood that was shed for you is life giving and that you are healed because our God is a God who give life not death…he is the river of life and you are not afraid because you belong to a conqueror. Anything that is trying to take away your life will flee from you…you will be set free by the blood of Jesus for nothing has any right to imprison you…or dominate your body and cause suffering nor death. You are healed in Jesus's name. He came so that you have life. Everything bow down to Jesus…evil surrenders and sets you free.

Psalm38:21-22

Do not abandon me, O LORD; do not stay away, my God! Help me now, O LORD my saviour!

- ❖ Continue to be firmly rooted in Christ the Lord; he takes away this cup of suffering from you for he already suffered on your behalf. He is with you always and do not despair, you will overcome.

Isaiah 40:31

But those who trust in the LORD for help will find their strength renewed.

- ❖ Trust is very important in your life, when you trust God you will find inner peace, the best way to receive from God is to trust him and know that he is mighty to save and that he will never fail you. Trusting God means you know that what he says comes to be and he will never fail you neither does he change or waver from his words of life he has spoken upon your life. Smile and be happy when words of hope are spoken in your live…be contented that it will come to be…that you are fine and that God is your strength and he is forever before you…ahead of you…he levels mountains for you, he makes everything easy for you so allow him in your life by trusting him. Trusting in God can pull down any strongholds in your life…trust means you have unshakable faith in God and nothing will lead you astray for you will instantly know that you will not be lost. You are found in Jesus and so remain strong in him. God loves you dearly. When overwhelmed by troubles and sickness call out to Jesus….for he is your hiding place.

Psalm 57:1-3

Be merciful to me, o God, be merciful, because I come to you for safety. In the shadow of your wings I find protection until the raging storms are over. I call to God the Most High, to God who supplies my every need. He will answer from heaven and save me; he will defeat my oppressors. God will show me his constant love.

- ❖ When you call upon the Lord, his sure help will come because you know his purpose in your life is to love you and help you and nurture you. God shows his power through us….we know we have a good and mighty God because he demonstrates his presence, love and power by healing us, protecting us, guiding us comforting us and being a trustworthy God. God`s goodness speaks for itself, he completely bring relief and rest where as the devil adds troubles to our lives. God shields us and blesses us. He brings complete joy and happiness. He does not bait…when healed by God it is complete healing and the sickness will never come back to take possession of your body. God is true and sure.

Psalm 33:18-19

The LORD watches over those who obey him, those who trust in his constant love. He saves them from death; he keeps them alive in times of famine.

- ❖ God will never let his own people perish; he stretches out his hands and rescues them against all odds. He nourishes them and they flourish with his good care. Do not be afraid when you are facing a downhill situation....you will soon rise and soar like an eagle. Trust in God all times and never lose hope. He is with you.

Psalm 54:1-2

Save me by your power, O God; set me free by your might! Hear my prayer, O God; listen to my words!

- ❖ Yeah...God will never get tired of hearing your voice and he will answer you by saving you. By crying out to him and acknowledging his mighty saving power, you are also praising and honouring him and evil will flee from you for you belong to God who is your redeemer, Satan cannot stay where God is praised, he hates it. And God is saying, "Be healed…be saved my child."

Isaiah 41:11-13

"Those who are angry with you will know the shame of defeat. Those who fight against you will die and will disappear from the earth. I am the Lord your God; I strengthen you and say, "Do not be afraid; I will help you.``

- ❖ No matter how aggressive and powerful the disease is in your body, no matter how dominant it has become over your life, it will be eradicated by the power of the living God…the blood of Jesus brought salvation and victory in our lives… suffering is a thing of the past in you. God is pouring out his healing from up above and every evil force in your life is being destroyed in the name of Jesus Christ our Saviour

Isaiah 49:15

"Can a mother forget the baby at her breast and have no compassion on the child she has borne? Though she may forget, I will not forget you!"

Psalm 37:23-24

The LORD guides a man in the way he should go and protect those who please him. If they fall, they will not stay down, because the LORD will help them up.

- ❖ Whatever you are going through on your bed because of sickness or trouble, it is not permanent, that illness will soon go because it has no place… and there is no room in your body for it to prevail, it will never win but be loosened….do not cry, do not panic, you will rise in the name of Jesus. You will shine like a star, like the sun and moon. You will be made strong again. No more pain and sorrow, no more grief but happiness.

Psalm 31:9-10

Be merciful to me, LORD, for I am in trouble; my eyes are tired from so much crying. I am completely worn out. I am exhausted by sorrow, and weeping has shortened my life. I am weak from all my troubles; even my bones are wasting away.

- ❖ Do not be down hearted …cheer up! God is with you. Do not lose hope…do not be afraid he is sure help…he is touching you right now and taking away this sorrow and pain in your life. He hears your groans and he listens to your prayers and heals you. God is our saviour and comfort. With him you are in a safe place.

Jeremiah 33:3

"Call to me, and I will answer you; I will tell you wonderful and marvellous things that you know nothing about."

- ❖ God never ceases to be amazing; he is a continuous source of our joy, honour and pride. He creates new beginnings for us, he surrounds us with his newness for us, and we have a new life in Jesus, life free of disaster and sickness, he is a God of all possibilities, he knows no defeat and will never surrender to anything, and he is the big power in our lives who makes the impossible disappear. When you are battling against "terminal illness," it seems like a death sentence has been passed on you. Hope is denied. But now in Jesus, this becomes your power, you will be able to shake off the harsh numbing pain of death and turn it into your power. You will overcome by the blood of Jesus, you will be successful you are being helped to beat it, and the world will be speechless in amazement. Our God is a wonder working God.

- ❖ God helps you not to escape this stronghold by succumbing to death, he will help you fight it and together with the Lord your journey will not end in darkness but leads to life. When people know about you, when they look at you, they do not nod to a death sentence anymore but to hope, to life. You will live long because God rescued you! He has chosen you to reveal his glory....Little one, stand up and walk...do not stagger! Be strong! Demonstrate his power in your life. God is great and wonderful.

Isaiah 41:14

The LORD says, "Small and weak as you are, Israel, don`t be afraid; I will help you. I the holy God of Israel am the one who saves you."

- ❖ God is for everyone, he does not choose according to greatness or power or strength and wealthy, he touches all; he makes even the smallest and most humble in families great. He is our God who is touching and bringing his holiness to little children, who are suffering and facing darkness, babies who do not even know how to ask from him except cry in pain...little babies...on the verge of death because they are feeble and small. Little one, you are significant to God and he is giving you back your valuable and deserving life. In God you speak, and he speaks for your life. He will not let the evil one wound you anymore; he is breaking the yoke of Satan and lifting you up in his glory and majesty. The harsh realities of disease and suffering is gone, this punishment you have endured is pushed away and completely removed. The devil`s chain of permanent oppression is removed and you are healed and found again. God is clothing you with his justice, victory and peace. Be bathed with the Holy Spirit. Be healed and be happy and bring peace back to your family...God has not forsaken you, he has loved you. Be completely healed in the name of Jesus.

Psalm 31:22

I was afraid and thought that he had driven me out of his presence. But he heard my cry, when I called to him for help.

❖ Do not be dismayed when you feel your prayers are not being answered...God will be working in ways you do not see, he will be already touching you and healing you when at the same time you feel healing or his answering hand is not coming. God is real and he hears your prayers and he does not forsake or ignore those who call out to him. He is our helper in all times. He is healing all the time.

Psalm 32:7

You are my hiding place; you will save me from trouble. I sing out aloud of your salvation because you protect me.

❖ You know when the hand of evil seems to be dominant in your life, when you are inflicted with the evil one, when you are constantly sick, suffering, attacked or when you are unhappy with your life, do not give up praying and asking for God`s mercy, your trouble is just temporary, you will pass through, you will be free from its clutches on your life, it is just trials of life, declare your salvation by leaning on God ...he is that place where you find peace and sanctuary, he is your safety, nothing can snatch you from the palms of our Lord and Master...our only God. Remember he gave us his Son whose hands, feet and side were pierced for your transgressions. He took away all our disgrace and he is our fortress. Our life is printed on his palms, we are a mark in him and we live in him and him in us. So do not be afraid for he is for you. Speak to him as your greatest friend and Father, tell him about all your sad feelings, all your fears, worries, all that is pressing you down, tell him you love him and he is your salvation, your only provider who will put things right for you because he has the power and ability...you will then feel his peace and light. You will experience a sense of freedom in reality. Do not be afraid.

Isaiah 41:17-20

" When my people in their need look for water, when their throats are dry with thirst, then I, the LORD , will answer their prayer; I, the God of Israel , will never abandon them. I will make rivers flow among barren hills and springs of water run in the valleys. I will turn the desert into pools of water and the dry land into flowing springs. I will make cedars grow in the desert, and acacias and myrtles and olive trees. Forests will grow in barren land, forest of pine and juniper and cypress. People will see this and know that

I, the LORD, have done it. They will come to understand that Israel`s God has made it happen"

- ❖ When we cry out to God...seeking his mercy... he responds and imparts life to us. Where there was hopelessness, there will be fulfilment; he fills up the void in our lives. Where there was no expectancy of life, he flourishes us with life and growth and healing and strength. The impossible is made possible with God`s love through Jesus Christ. There is hope in abundance and there is God`s favour in our lives. We overflow with life because God the creator is life, he creates life, and he restores life. We are forever happy because of our mighty saving God who is able, and we forever praise him and give him his deserving glory. There is no god like our healing, merciful, saving God...Creator of heaven and earth. He created all things beautiful and he never stops to sustain us. He made us live through his son Jesus Christ who died for us on the cross taking away death and sorrow. All that inhibit growth and life is demolished through the blood of Jesus. We are no longer arrested by disease and troubles; we are free and happy and live in peace. We are healed and we will always be healed, for Jesus is as he was yesterday, and is today and will be tomorrow. He healed before, he will heal now and forever, so cast down all your fear and live in hope.

Psalm 83:18

May they know that you alone are the LORD, supreme ruler over all the earth.

- ❖ God is easy to see, his works in our lives speaks for him. When you are healed of this disease then the whole world will praise him for his worthiness. When you are freed from the thing that is pressing you down, then you feel his relief. He is there to save us because he loves us and he has the command that drives out evil from your life, whatever trouble you are facing, it will be driven out by his authority and supernatural power…he is the one and only power that is quick to save in times of our needs. Nothing will terrify you anymore because you will know that there is a higher power that will break its force on your life. Do not be afraid. Praise him always!

Revelation 4:8

"Holy, holy, holy, is the Lord God Almighty, who was, who is, and who is to come".

1John3:21-22

If our hearts do not condemn us, we have confidence before God and receive from him anything we ask, because we obey his commands and do what pleases him.

- ❖ We are sure when we offer our prayers to God in the name of Jesus we will receive because that is why he died for us. He laid down his life so that we receive life in abundance, we receive life in its fullest, with all the things that adorns it, splendour, goodness, love, prosperity, and we are full in Christ. Be prepared to live, you will not die, you are a blessed child of God. He is taking away this weakness that is afflicting you. With a heart ready to receive, present your needs to God and you will not remain empty. He will fill you up.

1John 3:23

And this is his command: to believe in the name of his Son, Jesus Christ, and to love one another as he commanded us.

- ❖ Believe in Jesus Christ and you will be healed and saved! When you believe in Christ Jesus you are bringing him into you, when he is in you, then you have the power that drives out evil from your body. Your soul is saved and flesh and blood restored to perfection.

Isaiah 40:1

"Comfort, comfort my people," says your God.

- ❖ God wants us to be at peace all the time and his voice is there to tell us it is all well because he will be making your life to be filled with his goodness. He wants to show us he is our compassionate God and he will never leave us alone when we need him. His presence that brings relief and safety in our lives is very comforting. He just does not tell us to be at peace, God goes extra miles to put us at a peaceful position by his deeds, he correct the wrongs done to us, he pours out his blessings, he pave ways for us to break through, he mends the torn parts in our lives. He gives anything we ask and we are sure to receive. God is your comfort and be at peace with him, do not be afraid for he is always with you now, remember you are his, and he is your God.

Chapter 3

SALVATION COMES FROM THE LORD

John 3:16

For God loved the world so much that he gave his only Son, so that everyone who believes in him may not die but have eternal life.

- ❖ God loved us by having mercy on our sins and he gave us his only Son Jesus Christ to die on the cross for our transgressions. He atoned for us. We are forever reconciled with God and we are his children through Jesus Christ. When you believe in Jesus Christ as the Son of the living God who was sent as the Messiah, to save us and to redeem, then you will be set from bondage. The name Jesus brings healing and protection into our lives and we receive eternal life. We were bought back from sin through the blood of Jesus. We can never be condemned by Satan, we overcome by the blood and we are children of the light, and the light outshines darkness and therefore Jesus Christ is our bright shining light that changes our negative situations to become favourable. We are no longer walking in darkness because we are washed by his blood and we therefore receive the glory of the Lord. Let him in your life and be forever saved. Be healed in his name.

Mark 12:30

"Love the Lord your God with all your heart, with all your soul, with all your mind, and with all your strength. "

- ❖ The best thing to do to show love to God is to surrender your life to him. The most powerful reason is he is your Creator, a God who loves you and secondly instead of losing your life he healed you, he has mercy upon your life. He gave it back to you…he loved you. Love him back by giving him your life, that is acknowledge him first in everything you do, make him the lord of your life and live according to his ways. Know that God`s ways are good and upright. He is righteous and holy and when you surrender to him you also inherit his righteousness, you change all your ways and become a good child of God who waits upon him, who obeys him, who worship him alone as your personal Saviour. God is worthy... he gave you a second chance to life, he rescued you from the grave, and he wants you to live your life in the best and upright way. Cherish God`s love and goodness in your life by accepting him to lead you and guide you. Let him complete your new life for you are a new creation.

James 4:7-8

So then, submit to God. Resist the devil, and he will run away from you. Come near to God, and he will come near to you.

- ❖ Abstain from bad ways of life by giving your life to God; abstain from anything that is not Jesus. Apart from Jesus there is nothing good for you. When you live a prayerful life, a life that dwells in the word of God and all his ways, a life that seeks the lord`s leading, protection, goodness and his will in your life, then you will receive peace and rest. You will feel his guiding presence. The devil cannot attack you through sickness and suffering.

God protects you and cover you in the shadow of his mighty wings.

2 Samuel 22:5-7

The waves of death were all round me; the wave of destruction rolled over me. The danger of death was round me, and the grave set its trap for me. In my trouble I called to the LORD; I called to my God for help. In his temple he heard my voice; he listened to my cry for help.

John 3:17

For God did not send his Son into the world to be its judge, but to be its saviour.

- ❖ There is safety with Christ. There is mercy, there is grace and there is comfort. There is no fear but hope and happiness. There is complete salvation and completeness of everything in our lives. We are saved from any obstacles in our lives, from all kinds of danger, from unforeseen peril, from spiritual depletion, from physical harm, emotional harm; we are saved from financial harm. Even sickness can be used by the devil to rob a family financially, but God helps us through, he protects us from being emptied and from being surrounded by the whirlwind of troubles and difficulties brought during the time of sickness. In Jesus Christ, we are saved from poverty, we are saved from going under during these tempting times, he rescues us from sin of any kind, we become strong in faith and lean on him alone knowing he our saviour who died on the cross for us and nothing has never been able to defeat the power of the cross. Hence when we trust and cast all our troubles to him, we are saved from diseases and death, and we are saved from darkness. We are completely safe with God. When we reach out to him and tell ourselves that he is a God whom we can trust and that he is God who pulls out to his safety…to life we then receive help and we are healed in fullness.

Mark 10:14

"Let the children come to me, and do not stop them, because the kingdom of God belongs to such as these. "

- ❖ You are a special child of God and he cares for you. In God's heart, there is a sacred place and love for children. As a child you are a blessing from God and he cares for you in a very gentle way. You are safe with God, in Jesus's arm you are comfortable and secure. You are pure and innocent...you are beautiful...you are so divine. You are the joy of the world, you are the love of the world, rise and shine little one; God will heal you and help you to bud and blossom in your entire life. Glory, glory, glory to you...The lord is with you and be healed in the name of Jesus.

Psalm 23:4

Even if I go through the deepest darkness, I will not be afraid, Lord, for you are with me. Your shepherd`s rod and staff protect me.

- ❖ No matter how deep or how wide your trouble is, whether you are facing death, God is with you and will rescue you, he will lift you from that pit he will take away the oppressing obstacle and lift you up high above. God brings healing; do not give up keep holding on for he is with you. God gave us his Son Jesus so that we conquer all things that oppress us. We conquer the stronghold of sickness.

Psalm 33:9

When he spoke, the world was created; at his command everything appeared.

- ❖ Nothing defeats God, when he gives command for the disease to go, it will be cured. God is Supreme and Holy, nothing disobey God when he commands diseases and all darkness to go, the devil and his demons flee, trouble leaves you, suffering cannot gain control on you, you are instantly freed. When God speaks, miracles happen. There is movement; God stirs events for the betterment of his creation. God is a super power in your life who will rescue you miraculously, where hope is denied…God brings it, he speaks of it, he breathes it into you, he breathes life to your body. Breathe in the name of Jesus!

Psalm 34:18

The Lord is near to those who are discouraged; he saves those who have lost all hope.

❖ In your weakest moment....when you have resigned to the stronghold of death....when you feel nothing will change your circumstances... when you have accepted what you call "fate" then God speaks life unto you...there is no "fate" but you have full blessings...you have purpose in life....you have a destiny created by God himself and he wants you to live a long and happy life and you are healed in every area of your life. "Stand up and walk and sing Hallelujah in jubilation!" says the Lord God Almighty.

1John 3:22

We receive from him whatever we ask, because we obey his commands and do what pleases him.

❖ When we receive Jesus and believe that he is the Son of our living God who came to save us, then whatever we ask from God in the name of Jesus we will receive because we are accepting and acknowledging God's love for us and his encouragement in him. For the glory of God is seen through his Son Jesus Christ our Saviour. Believe and be healed in the name that is higher than every name, be healed in the name of Jesus.

Psalm 70:5

I am weak and helpless; come to me quickly, O God. You are my saviour LORD-hurry to my aid!

- ❖ Speak out your troubles and God hears you…say it all out…tell it all to him…ask for his help, do not feel restrained just pour out your heart to the Lord and he will set you free. Do not carry this burden alone give it all to Jesus Christ our saviour and he will set you free. It's not your fight, it's not your war, Jesus is your king and he will win this battle for you. Whatever is pressing you down bows down to Jesus and surrender its dwelling in your body. Let it go…let it out…speak out and be heard! Be freed in the name above every name. Be free from anxiety and fear, be freed from powerlessness. He is saying to you, "Here I am, I am your strength and triumph you are saved and healed in my name".

Isaiah 60:19

"No longer will the sun be your light by day or the moon be your light by night; I, the LORD, will be your eternal light, the light of my glory will shine on you. Your days of grief will come to end. I, the Lord, will be your eternal light. More lasting than the sun and moon. "

- ❖ God gave us his only Son Jesus Christ and through him we receive the glory of God, through Jesus, our sins are pardoned, we have a happy and safe life, he is our eternal light. If we ask God for anything in the name of Jesus we will not be denied. He will grant us our request for through him all things are possible. Through Jesus we receive eternal life, everything holds together for us through him. We have order and peace not chaos. It is all bright and beautiful. There is nothing God cannot handle for us through his Son. He is the tree of life. Receive Jesus and be saved. He is your supreme power, the Rock that is higher than anything in your entire life.

3John 1:2

My dear friend, I pray that everything may go well with you and that you may be in good health- as I know you are well in spirit.

- ❖ May God heal you physically, spiritually and emotionally! Be completely healed in the name of Jesus, the name above every name...the name that brings success to you. The name that breaks strongholds and saves you! He is your conquest. We break the yoke of suffering in the name of Jesus. Be healed little one.

Chapter 4

HE CARES

Isaiah 40:27-31

Israel, why then do you complain that the LORD doesn`t know your troubles or care if you suffer injustice. Don`t you know? Haven`t you heard? The LORD is the everlasting God; he created all the world. He never grows tired or weary. No one understands his thoughts. He strengthens those who are weak and tired. Even those who are young grow weak; young men can fall exhausted. But those who trust in the Lord for help will find their strength renewed. They will rise on wings like eagles; they will run and not get weary; they will walk and not grow faint.

- ❖ It is well with you, you do not deserve to be in pain or suffer any troubles…you are a valuable child of God and he is right inside you…taking away your misery. God created you therefore every part of you does not escape his healing flow. You will overcome, you will breakthrough. Even though in flesh you are broken, God is never broken, he continuously stands by you and through him you are strong and will help you with his power for success. You will soar like an eagle in your new life God is restoring. Nothing will bring you down; you will prosper in the name of Jesus.

Psalm 68:19-20

Praise the Lord who carries our burdens day after day; he is the God who saves us. Our God is a God who saves; he is the Lord, our Lord, who rescues us from death.

- ❖ Jesus came into the world so that death may die and through him you have your life...the devil cannot steal it....he uses disease to put you down, to break you ...but disease is under the feet of Jesus and he helps us to crush it under our feet, by trusting in the Lord God Almighty as our undefeated healer and Saviour, we receive strength and restoration. We are healed.

Revelation 4:11

"Our Lord and God! You are worthy to receive glory, honour, and power. For you created all things and by your will they were given existence and life. ``

- ❖ Because God does only good things for us... when we are weak he helps us to be strong and confident, hopeful and be at peace, he is therefore a symbol of all the good things you can ever want in your life. Think of all the wonderful things that you love and surround yourself with them; think of the stars, the smiling moon, the bright shining sun, the glorifying light the green earth, the beautiful blooming flowers with different bright and beautiful colors, think of your favourite pets , animals, birds....all is just beautiful and that is what God wants your life to be like, he wants you surrounded with beauty, he created all these things for your benefit...so that you enjoy life...and he created you to live it to the fullest. Just remember you are going to live long and happy in Christ because he died for us so that our lives bosom...remove darkness from your path by reaching out to Jesus, call out his name and praise God for your life, tell him how awesome he is ...how wonderful and how beautiful he is, then the way you describe him, the way you perceive as your God and the way you praise him; is the way your life will be like because God is also in you. Remember what God created; he loved and because he loves; then he cares greatly. He is a great and supernatural merciful God. No one can be like him.

Psalm 43:5

Why am I so sad? Why am I so troubled? I will put my hope in God, and once again I will praise him, my saviour and my God.

- ❖ With God there is no fear of disaster, there is no loss, and there is no oppression, you will not fail, you will be fine. Trust in God and be at peace with him. Your praise for him will not change because each day you will see great changes coming from him alone. He is a God of improvement and restoration. Give him all your burdens, give them to Jesus, and because he cares, he will never forsake you, your prayers will surely be answered and he will give you rest completely. He will bring healing in your life. He is your hope and he will fulfil his promise that he came for us to live in complete happiness, to have trouble free life and to live glorifying God for the good work of his hands in our lives through Jesus Christ our saviour. Ask for anything in the name of Jesus and God will supply it to you. That is God`s heart for us.

Isaiah 43:11-12

"I alone am the LORD, the only one who can save you. I predicted what would happen, and then I came to your aid."

- ❖ Whatever happens in our lives, all the difficulties we encounter, God knows and see and by his power and will, we are rescued. When he speaks life in us, when he tells us we will be healed, then he goes on to heal us. When he tells us there is hope for us, he then goes on to create that hope for us. He gave us hope by giving us his Son Jesus Christ for our salvation. We live because he allows us to by his grace and mercy. God is everywhere at one time, nothing escapes his attention. Whatever presses you down, God never fails to put right. He is your power that will help you pull through and crush those trials of illness and suffering. God is the only power that breaks evil completely and brings victory. He is not a God who tries, he does, he is sure, he knows, he is our superpower and there is no other god that will save you except him who created the world. It is God`s sovereignty that gives you existence. No one can steal it from you. You are blessed and safe.

Isaiah 51:3

"I will show compassion to Jerusalem to, to all who live in her ruins. Though her land is a desert, I will make it a garden, like the garden I planted in Eden. Joy and gladness will be there and songs of praise and thanks to me."

- ❖ Even though your body has deteriorated, even if there is no more coordination in you internal organs, even if the codes for your existence are almost broken, even if your whole system is shutting down, do not be afraid God will restore you to life, he will give you your beauty, you will soon blossom like flower, you are being revived to life and in the name of Jesus believe you are healing…you will rise and shine. Little one; be healed and praise the Lord your God who is mighty to save and who is undefeated. Every difficulty your family is going through because of this illness, all problems they are facing, God will ease them; God will lighten their struggles as well and also completely heal you. You will bring happiness in their hearts and they will see the glory of the Lord through you. God will sustain them, he will re-fill them instead of empting them because God is very near to those who are helpless and hopeless. The fears that are causing their brokenness will be removed from their path because God who is healing will bring peace and relief. He will make everything beautiful, you will bud and blossom little one. You have a beautiful life ahead, and you will pull through because you belong to God.

Isaiah 51:15

"I am the LORD your God; I stir up the sea and make its waves roar. My name is the LORD Almighty."

- ❖ This is a sure declaration of his power and ability. There is complete authority in the Lord your God; powerful ruling that gives us the satisfaction that in truth we are safe with him. He is King of everything, the sea is deep and scary and when it is shaken, hell breaks out, it swallows and takes everything down, it conquers mankind, but it is only God himself who have the power to calm it. He controls everything and knows how to stop all raging forces in our lives without doubt. Even when you are facing extremely heavy and dark storms in your life, when there is an upheaval and firestorms in your lives, when all hope is lost; God has a way of calming them for you.

Call out his name, reach out to him, cry to your God and he will fight your battle and you will be above it. You will overcome, you will not go down, and you are anchored by the power of the Holy Spirit, our God and victor. Call upon his supreme and holy name. Do not suffer in silence; and do not let anyone or anything block you from receiving your healing, keep asking and surrounding yourself with God`s presence. Pray, sing in your heart, praise him, call upon the blood of Jesus for protection and completion in healing, ask for life not death, sent it away from you, tell it you are a child of a life giving God and be firm about it, for you surely have a powerful God who is able to restore you. His healing power is absolute.

There are no limits with God, there are no boundaries. He crosses everything and breaks every power in this universe; his merciful loving name is Mighty God, Everlasting Father,

Prince of peace, our only God who is grand and impressive in our lives and in everything he does...we call upon his help and we receive it. Yes, that's why he has a glorious name. His name exudes power, his name is majestic, his name is victorious, his name is awesome and all wonder filling, his name is healing, and he is love and peace. God is beautiful. God is not vain; there is hope and success in him for us. Whatever we ask for, whatever we anticipate from him, whatever we completely hope for from him, and whatever we wait for, in understanding and knowing we have asked from an able God; we ultimately receive. God never fails. Nothing can stop his endless love for us. Do not give up, you are safe and healthy because you belong to a competent God who has sole knowledge of all that he created, no one can outrun God, no one, can play God. No one is wiser than God. Put in your heart the fact that God is your defender, your hope, your help and your trust and shield. He is the Lord Almighty Rock eternal and we say, "Hallelujah to the highest."

Chapter 5

JESUS, MY ROCK

Psalm 42:8

May the LORD show his constant love during the day, so that I may have a song at night, a prayer to the God of my life.

- ❖ It is good to continue to ask favour from our God because you know he is a higher power than you and you are respecting and welcoming his love in your life and when you sing to God, his happiness is poured down on you...you are praising and asking for his glory to shine forever in your life. You are dwelling in his presence and nothing can go wrong, your everyday walk with him, is a peaceful walk because you are anchored by the power of the living God. He knows when and how to pour out his favour, and how to renew and protect you. It is by his Spirit alone that you will be above and not beneath. You will be healed and be replenished. Do not lose hope. Hold fast to your faith that God will rescue you in the name of Jesus. Believe that day by day he is by your side, you will not be disgraced.

Psalm 18:1-2

How I love you, LORD! You are my defender. The LORD is my protection; he is my strong fortress. My God is my protection, and with him I am safe. He protects me like a shield; he defends me and keeps me safe.

- ❖ God is the love of your heart, the love of your life, when you are down, facing difficulties, you do not need to work hard or fight hard to be healed, God is easy, and mighty to save.....he does everything for you, all you have to do is call out to him, reach out to you because he takes care of you, remind him that you know that he is looking after you and he is your only helper, there is no one else to turn to when you are facing death and there seems to be no hope for your life to continue.....with God there is hope, he is strong and mighty and he shields you from being taken down. He is supernaturally above everything, when he says be healed no one refutes him, we cannot doubt his true unchanging word…God is the final and only answer to your life troubles and all your cares.

Psalm 18:28

O LORD, you give me light; you dispel my darkness.

- ❖ Be healed and walk in the light of God. Be forever his shining star all your life and remember to praise the Lord to enable him. He will give you his virtue and his will for your life will glow forever. You are in the hands of good, you belong to what is worth, you are a product of a highly esteemed power, and whatever you do, or whatever befalls on you will result in merit. When you face troubles…people will speak about how God miraculously intervened and saved you, when you are ill, you become an example of God`s love to his children, God will create a story of his supremacy and holiness through you. Most importantly you cause glorification of a mighty and unchallenged power, you cause people to praise Jesus Christ our Lord who died for us on the cross so that we conquer death through him. You are a success story in Jesus`s name. God loved us by sacrificing his Son for us on the cross, and when we embrace Jesus as our personal saviour, he comes with healing and power in your life. Remember he is the light that took away our darkness, our grief, our troubles and desolation. We are not banished in anguish to despair.

Psalm 18:30-32

This God- how perfect are his deeds! How dependable his words! He is like a shield for all who seek his protection. The LORD alone is God; God alone is our defence. He is the God who makes me strong, who makes my pathway safe.

- ❖ God never lies …whatever he speaks of in your life comes to be, whatever he declares cannot be change for our God is a God who does not waver, he does not change, he remains the same loving, truthful, wonderful, compassionate God. He is everlasting. No other power is above him, no human is above God. We are his children who seek his love and guidance in everything we do. When we give our lives to God it means that we trust him; and his truthfulness is what we are anchoring our lives on. We praise him because he will never fail and shame us...he is forever true, dependable and merciful...we are surefooted with God. We have a solid foundation, and we are standing on solid ground that will never shake. So, "Be still and know he is God" he is praised upon heavens and earth because of his faithfulness and triumph. He comes into your life to give you strength, healing, love and complete hope.

Psalm 18:46

The LORD lives! Praise my defender! Proclaim the greatness of the God who saves me.

- ❖ God is real...he is not just a mental picture we formulate in our minds, nor is he a deity that we need to fix our beliefs on, just for the sake of having faith to depend on something in our lives. God wants you truthful heart, he does not want you to try him. Believe in him and love him with all your life because he is true, God is living and active, he is Spirit and upright, he moves, he speaks, his eyes are everywhere...he is not an image nor a vacuum...we are created in his likeness as beings. When Jesus Christ came on earth, born of the virgin Mary and the Holy Spirit, he was made human and God`s Spirit was upon him. He performed great miracles, he was flawless, he saved lives, and he spoke of his Father in heaven who had sent him to do his will for us his children, that is, to die for us so that we live complete lives, and have eternal life. God`s love for us was manifested in Jesus Christ his only begotten Son. God was therefore made visible through his Son Jesus. God showed his great and matchless love for us by sacrificing him for our sins and we forever praise him because we know that anything we ask our Father in heaven, in the name of his Son Jesus, we receive. We now belong to the light not darkness. Praise the Lord!

Psalm18:16

The LORD reached down from above and took hold of me; he pulled me out of the deep waters.

- ❖ There are times when you feel you have sunk so deep in your pain, disease and trouble and there seem to be no hope, you feel you are travelling a lonely journey where there is no turning back and you have reached that point of acceptance, when you say to yourself, "so be it," "I have had enough and I no longer care whether I fall, let it be." At this point of dire weakness and surrender, God stretches out his hand making it very visible... this is the point when he has actually reached to you and bless you with his favour, he turns your situation around favourably and pulls you out of your predicament, he pulls you from death, you suddenly breathe, you suddenly walk, you suddenly lost the pain that was terrible and stubborn, you suddenly stopped bleeding, you suddenly felt free and calm, you suddenly came to reality and could connect with your environment, that shaking left you, that fear went down and was replaced by smiles and contentment, that low feeling of despair disappeared, that emptiness was filled and that loneliness was removed and only God`s love is shown by all those people around you sharing your joy... sharing the happiness of your miracle...anything that was oppressing you flees and there is only good news from you...your doctor, your parents and all your friends are happy with you..suddenly you are a person again...you are no longer smiling upon death...you are no longer welcoming it... you have defeated it...you have shamed darkness in the name of Jesus, he has brought healing, and salvation and that is why we say, " a miracle took place." We did not see with our human eyes our

God working for our salvation; he was there with us all the time. We wish we had trusted him all along...but we are human and weak, and God`s truthfulness speaks out for him. His ways... his works demonstrate that he is a holy and powerful God. Take away that shame and praise God, respect him, exalt him, glorify his name then you continue to receive his everlasting mercies... he will continue to walk with you, blessing you each day, he will be healing you in every area of your life. He will show you new things and create them for you. God`s pulling power is forever for us his children. When he pulls us out of trouble, then if we honour him, he lifts us up high above. Some people when they are blessed...when they receive God`s healing....they completely forget about him and go on with their ways as if God never touched them, they forget about his good deeds until they encounter trouble again and they run back to him because even if they are lost in the world, they know the truth that God is the highest power and in him there is mercy and forgiveness. God never rejects us and when we surrender to him we will be complete, no harm will come our way, that is what he promises us in Psalm 91:9-11" You have made the LORD your defender, the Most High your protector and so no disaster will strike you, no violence will come near your home. God will put his angels in charge of you to protect you wherever you go."

Ephesians 6:16

At all times carry faith as a shield; for with it you will be able to put out all the burning arrows shot by the evil one.

- ❖ When you believe that you will be healed and saved by the power of the Holy Spirit, that you will not die, that the blood of Jesus gives you life and salvation, then nothing will hinder the flow of God`s peace and love that comes from his throne. The devil makes you doubt...at the devil`s sceptre, you start to look at the depth of your problem, your sickness, your troubles and feel there is no hope and then sink and succumb to the pains of your illness, you let it take its toll on you and this is what the world of the devil is composed of. You allow yourself to go in the abyss with him where there is endless despair, but if you defy the chains of sickness, the chains of Satan by declaring that you will be healed and that God will never abandon you to the grave; when you continuously speak words of healing in your life and call out to God as your saviour in prayers, it will be well with your soul...you shall live and not die; because you believe, therefore it will come to be. Remember when creating the universe God spoke without doubt or hesitation what he had willed, he spoke full of wisdom, knowledge and understanding that what he was speaking would come to be....therefore it came to be, it took place, it really happened. Speak healing in your life do not give up or hesitate, do not listen to words that make you feel low and down, do not take negativity even from other people, keep hoping, and this is between you and God, this is you and hope, this is your own cry to a wonderful and able God who exonerates, this is your moment with God alone in the name of Jesus. You will receive, your hope will be realised. Have complete faith that is unshakable, do not let the devil penetrate into your heart, this is the time for you to see God alone, it's your journey that will take you to a place full of life and growth, it's your awakening...it will not end in death for you are being healed. Beat it...overcome in the name of Jesus. Amen!

Psalm 19:14

May the words of my mouth and the meditation of my heart be pleasing in your sight, O LORD, my Rock and my Redeemer.

- ❖ Whatever you are going through, do not be angry with God, do not pour insult or your fury on him…be gentle with yourself as well as with God , be humble because he sees your affliction and he knows what is in your heart, he knows what is grieving you, he knows all your frustration, God does not cause illness, troubles, difficulties, they are just trials upon your life caused by the evil one and we therefore see God`s love and faithfulness when he has helped us to overcome. God proved to Satan that darkness will never win over the children of light. Where ever you are know that God is for you and will never be against you. Your illness will cause glorification of God`s presence in your live when he heals you…you will praise him not the devil. Rather cry out to him as in Jeremiah 17:14 "LORD, heal me and I will be completely well; rescue me and I will be perfectly safe. You are the one I praise!`` Think of God in his saving ways and what other miracles he did for other people, he will also do for you. If he healed; then you will also be healed,

God can do it for you because you are his special child whom he loves. You are very important to God and he wants what is best for you in his Godly way...in his goodness. Make yourself lesser than God...he is above you and he has mercy for you. If you are a parent...going through the pain your child is going through, feeling hopelessness, speak to God about the exact way you are feeling, whether you feel helpless, stranded, and you feel your life has suddenly come to a halt, you feel your situation is not changing for the better, you feel you are losing, tell it as it is to God. He is pleased to hear your cries to him; he is pleased to know that you look up to him as a higher power that can set you free. There is no other God than our Creator, the true God, he is there to help us in our times of need, and we are at a safe place with him. Get rid of fear. Do not lean on your own ways because as human you are prone to human error. Money will not buy life for you or your child but the Spirit of the living God can set you free and bring healing. Reach out to him and ask God to cover your child with the blood of Jesus for healing and protection. The blood of Jesus never fails.

Romans 8:35

Who, then, can separate us from the love of Christ? Can trouble do it, or hardship or persecution or hunger or poverty or danger or death?

- ❖ There is sympathy and mercy for our lives in Christ. He took away condemnation by washing our sins by his blood. No one can sentence us to death because the living power of God is upon us, the Spirit of our Sovereign God is Fathering us.

Romans 8:37-39

No, in all these we have complete victory through him who loved us! For I am certain that nothing can separate us from his love: neither death nor life, neither angels nor other heavenly rulers or powers, neither the present nor the future, neither the world above nor the world beneath- there is nothing in all creation that will ever be able to separate us from the love of God which is ours through Christ Jesus our Lord.

- ❖ Your life might seem shattered and scattered all over, but God is picking up all those broken pieces and putting them together, he is mending you and healing you, nothing stops him, nothing can undo what he has already done, nothing can shake him because he loves you. Be healed in the highest name of Jesus!

Isaiah 43:13

"I am God and always will be. No one can escape from my power; no one can change what I do."

- ❖ Listen to the voice of God, the voice of healing and saving. Accept his power in your life and be victorious. Experience his supreme ways by worshiping him; and turning to him alone in all your life, in joy and in struggles. God is your inevitable victory.

Psalm 98:1

Sing a new song to the LORD; he has done wonderful things! By his own power and holy strength he has won the victory.

Chapter 6
IT'S POSSIBLE WITH GOD.

Mark 10:27

Jesus looked straight at them and answered, "This is impossible for man, but not for God; everything is possible for God. ``

- ❖ Do not be overwhelmed by how difficult and complicated your situation is; do not be scared by the names like "terminal illness," they are just names without power, names to put you down, do not be close knitted with that problem. You may be told you are terminally ill and be told you have a month to live, six months, a year or two, you may be told you have reached a point where nothing on this earth can be done to save you from death....you may be told you have reached the end, you may be told earnestly that you have reached a dead end.... deny it, defy this stronghold and hold on to the garment of Christ, cling to Jesus, for he is your hope, he came to save those who are completely lost, he came so that the hopeless have hope. There is mercy and compassion in him and surely he will save you in his mighty name. Do not take the world`s judgement, they tell you , you are dead before you die but life comes from God if you reach out to him, do not be afraid, even if there is the smell of death on your bed and linen, you will rise in the name of Jesus and you will be completely healed. You will live to praise the Lord, you will live to lift up his name, he will raise you and this disease will not end in death. Receive your miracle in the name that is above every name, the name that brings victory, the name that conquers all. Be whole again in the name of Jesus. May the Spirit of the holy God bring healing and favour in your life. He is a God of divine intervention; he is our glorious supernatural God. He is holy, holy, holy! He is a faithful and gracious God. He is a God of possibilities, a God who raised his only son from death and conquered once and for all, he is a God who defeats all obstacles, he has no boundaries, he has no limits....God heals and believe this, there is nothing that cannot be cured by God, terminal illness is just a term used to bury people before they actually die, it sounds fearful, it shows how desperate we have become, we have surrendered to its torture, but there is hope in the Lord, there hope in Christ Jesus, Believe in him and you will be saved. God created the whole world and nothing can be deemed impossible. He is enthroned up high above, he is Lord over all and he is the Lord of our lives.

Galatians 5:1

Freedom is what we have –Christ has set us free! Stand, then, as free people, and do not allow yourselves to become slaves again.

- ❖ You are set free from all bondage through Jesus, defy being captive of disease, being captive of condemnation, and defy the yoke of evil. It does not belong to you. You are a child of light, a child of life, the very successful child of God. Be upright in all your ways and thinking and you are made complete through Jesus Christ your Saviour. Be set free from sickness in the name of Jesus…. May the Lord `s truthful ways give you strength and show his will in your life by showing you your purpose for existence. May he equip you with knowledge and understanding, may his wisdom guide you and may he grant complete healing in your life and help you in your entire life.

Ephesians 6:17

And accept salvation as a helmet, and the word of God as the sword which the Spirit gives you.

- ❖ You received freedom through Jesus...you were saved. Use the word of God to close any window that can let the devil in your life. Read your bible, speak out what you read, put it in your heart and meditate upon his word in your life. Trouble will come to pass and that is sure. When you use the word of God, any alien that has gained entry into your body will flee, they will say goodbye for light and darkness cannot mix. There is havoc with Satan, he is a mess in your life, he brings confusion, disarray, and he brings disorder, sickness, turmoil and deception. The devil is corrupt and deceives you about your situation, he makes you feel worse than ever and lead you to hope for the worst, he does not allow anything good for you, let your mind dwell on Jesus instead and all his bright ways, turn away from fear and think positive about your life. Jesus is sincere in all his ways. Satan is an unashamed hypocrite, he steals our lives through devious ways but God is light, he sees everything that the fraudulent devil uses to destroy us. God rises to save, Satan cannot compete with our truthful, faithful and righteous God; he is forever losing the battle. God`s eyes sees through darkness and darkness is outshined, it is completely removed and it becomes ineffective, it becomes vain and powerless. Satan cannot harm you when you have drawn nearer to God. He can no longer lie to you because you are a product of what is clean and upright and majestic in all ways, you are covered by the glory of God, you are protected by the blood of Jesus. The devil cannot bring his ailments and prevail, he cannot make you suffer anymore, he cannot use anyone against you to win your soul, and all fails because the power of the living God is forever before you. The bible was inspired by God and he breathed his word and when it comes to us we inhale his breath and we live by it and we overcome. Make it your daily bread because it is full of light. The word of God opens your eyes and ears to the presence of his saving power. Make your life easy, claim your light and fill your body with it. Hear the word of God and understand what he is saying to you and feel his moving power to heal you and protect you from all your troubles. Remove all doubt and trust in God alone. It will all come to pass; you will be fine, you will be well and completely be in good health. This is a sure promise. Once God heals you, disease will never come back to you; it is done and finished in the name of Jesus.

Jeremiah 17:14

Heal me, O LORD, and I will be healed; save me and I will be saved, for you are the one I praise.

- ❖ We pray to God for healing and saving when we are in trouble...even when we are facing the toughest times of our lives, we do not run to the devil, we do not seek other gods except our Only One Living true God, we praise him alone and therefore we understand that God does not lie, what he promises he fulfils and when we ask from him we receive in truth and in Spirit. No one can help the way God does; his ways are just and true, faithful and merciful. We are healed and we are saved in the name of Jesus! We praise him alone, we give him his glory, and no other power can steal what we in turn offer to our God; we give our lives to him, we lay our lives before him; for he is the God who has loved us and there is no other God like him.

Isaiah 44:6

The LORD, who rules and protects Israel, the Lord Almighty, has this to say: "I am the first, the last, the only God: there is no other god but me"

- ❖ Salvation comes from God alone; we have no other source of healing except from the living God who enables us. Some people when diagnosed with diseases that are categorised as terminal..... they panic, in their panic they run around seeking other modes of healing believing they will receive it, some go to psychics and sought occult healing, some go for herbs from different kinds of sources, people run all over the world seeking people who claim to have healing powers, they seek superhuman powers and Knowledge, they delve in ideologies, scientific ways, witchcraft powers and all kinds of spiritual ways. But there is only one way, one God and his healing, there is only one medium to God who intercedes for us when we are empty and overwhelmed with difficulties, and that medium is Jesus Christ, help comes through him alone, apart from him there is nothing, permanent healing comes from God and in Jesus`s name we receive his mercy. Again some people fool themselves believing that anything that relieves their pain is good, it is deceiving, it is temporary, in fact the victim becomes worse than ever in a short period, that system they have depended upon made everything worse and Eventually death engulfs them. Stick to Jesus and live, his ways are easy, the only fundamental rule is to trust in him alone, be single minded, focus on the things of God alone and shun the world's mystic ideologies.....Do away with double minded. People who are two faced, accept God's promises and they seek his ways and when they get impatient and feel desperate they also seek other gods, and other ways....they think it is fine to deal with two schools of thought but the result is doom, there is no life but death. Do not mix God with evil; do not drink from the cup of the Lord and at the same time drink from the cup of demons. Have a solid bond with Jesus Christ, belong to the blood that was shed to bring your salvation... through the blood of Jesus we are saved and by his wounds we are healed. The truth is there is no other God except the one who created the world and gave up his only begotten Son for our transgression and that through him we receive joy and happiness. He is taking away your pain, your sickness and carrying it and healing you, he is setting you free from bondage. Love God with all your life, do not move to the right or to the left....focus on Christ, stick to salvation.

I Corinthians 10: 21

You cannot drink from the lord's cup and also from the cup of demons; you cannot eat at the Lord's table and also at the table of demons.

❖ Worship the one and only God. He is Omnipotent, Omnipresent and Omniscient. There is no other God beside him for you and me. The devil and his ways have no room in our lives. Praise and worship your one and only God. Do not seek other worldly means for help; the devil can lure you to try other interests just to claim you. There is one God, whom you pray to, honour him by offering your prayers to him alone. Lean on his understanding and peace and love alone. Follow his ways, be straight-forward and sanctified in all your ways. Avoid all that is bad and evil by surrendering to God alone and trust that in the name of Jesus we receive mercy and the love that comes from our God in heaven who reigns in justice and peace and who will help us through, he will rescue us in our times of need and he will always be with us and will forever help us. He is our light, our Father, and we are his own children purchased by the blood of Jesus, therefore we have victory, and the devil or troubles cannot win. Beat that fear in you and embrace Jesus. He died for you to live in happiness and fullness. We belong to a defeating God who is virtuous. His ways are forever clean and upright and he helps us to be like him by the power of the Holy Spirit. As his children whom he saved from condemnation through the blood of Jesus, we are made holy and righteous in all our ways and he helps us to overcome, to be survivors not losers. We will not be submerged but we will rise.

Isaiah 43:11

"I alone am the LORD, the only one who can save you. ``

- ❖ God does not keep it as a secret that he is the only God and that He is the only one to save you. Only God can bring change and life, apart from him there is nothing except death. Seek the Lord and live, do not be fooled by the world, do not be led astray by any forces, do not be afraid to have allegiance to your only God, he is worthy because he saves you and because he moves for your life. He refreshes your soul and brings peace in your life. Know that he protects you from all threats and the evil one. Revere God and proclaim his glory and majestic ways.

Psalm 100:2

Never forget that the LORD is God, he made us and we belong to him; we are his people, we are his flock.

❖ We belong to him; he is the supreme power that shields us. He guides us and he rescue us like lost lambs. We are in his safe hands.

Mark 12:30

"Love the Lord your God with all your heart, with all your soul, with all your mind, and with all your strength. ``

❖ In everything you do, put God first, and worship him alone. Completely surrender to him then you will receive his victories in your life. Do not envy the things of this world, wait upon your God and receive from him. Be devoted completely to the Lord your God, when you praise him, do so with all your heart…let every word you say be true. Then you will have a meaningful relationship with Him.

Luke 8:50

"Don`t be afraid; only believe, and she will be well."

❖ Do not panic when God says you will be fine and when he says you are healed, believe, have faith in him that he knows and he is able to save. Every word of God will never remain empty, it is fulfilled...when God speaks there is purpose, because he is supreme and majestic. When he created the world he spoke and what he spoke was not lost but was realised...every single word of God has its own meaning in our lives...God is not there to play games of fallacy. He is the truth, the "I Am.`` meaning he is real, living and Almighty, Sovereign and Holy. Believe in the saving power of God.

Mark 11:24

"For this reason I tell you: when you pray and ask for something, believe that you have received it, and you will be given whatever you ask for. ``

❖ There is power in faith and belief in God`s capabilities. He is our Father who knows the needs of his children and will fulfill them. Therefore keep hoping, your anticipation will be rewarded. God will not crush your hope; he will satisfy your request. He will fulfill your wishes.

Isaiah 41:10

"Do not be afraid- I am with you! I am your God- let nothing terrify you! I will make you strong and help you; I will protect you and save you. ``

- ❖ God takes away all fear and gives you his blessings. He is a soothing God and his ways are easy to see because they reveal his power for us and his strength that we inherit, he carries us and we feel good and comforted, that all is well with us and that we are at a right place with him. We are made strong. God in his highness has mercy for us...he speaks gentle and healing words to us, he is not harsh, he is forever kind to his children for he will not let us sink low in our troubles, he forgives us and heal our diseases and rescue us from troubles. He puts a hedge of protection around us and we find his peace. God is your place of safety.

John 8:12

Jesus spoke to the Pharisees again, "I am the light of the world, `` he said, "Whoever follows me will have the light of life and will never walk in darkness. "

- ❖ Jesus is our Saviour, Comforter, and Redeemer. He leads us to safe places all the time. Remember he died for you on the cross so that you have light, hope, joy, peace and a trouble free life. We are cleansed by his blood and we walk a holy walk with him...we live a blameless life free from Satan`s luring ways....free from evil...it cannot come near those who are covered by the blood of Jesus. Darkness fails to prosper in the lives of those covered by the blood of Jesus. Jesus is upholding us.

John 14:1

"Do not let your hearts be troubled. Trust in God; trust also in me.``

- ❖ Why would you be troubled when you are covered under the wings of our mighty God...believe that he is saying "nothing will break you...nothing will take you away from my peace, comfort and security." You were bought by the blood of our King Jesus, who helps and protects us...when you offer prayers to God , come before him in the name of his Son Jesus for he is our intermediary before God....through him we receive healing and he is a shield for us in our battles with life.

Trust that he is always with you and will help you, and lift your heart to him. The burdens of life you are carrying are not yours but his…so give them to him in prayer and he will give you relief, he takes away our sorrows, he bore our diseases and through him we are saved, we are healed. You will be released from this bondage…. you are no longer confined in sickness, this illness is not yours, surrender it to our God the Father in the Name of His Son Jesus and be healed completely! Amen.

Zechariah 4:6

"Not by might nor by power, but by my Spirit." says the LORD Almighty.

- ❖ It is only through the love and power of God that you will overcome, there is nothing you can do to help yourself except praying and seeking his face….seek his eyes, when he looks at you, you will be fine, seek his mercy always…reach out to him and only him alone will heal you, he alone will help you cross the bridge for he will be with you, he alone will break through for you, and he alone will win your battle. When you are battling against terminal illness, against death, its only

God`s power to save that we should reach out and he agrees with us that, it is only him who can show us his mercy and love and set you free from the shame of death. Your powerful connections with people with influential positions cannot help, your powerful position in this world is futile, and your money or special talents cannot rescue you from incurable ailments, only the Spirit of God, supernatural, holy and almighty can help you. The Spirit of the living Lord is upon you, helping you to re-surface. He will win this battle for you and you will live because he is saying "Live... breathe." You will be able because of his ability to heal and rescue. He is your hiding place, your fortress, your Rock, your deliverer and power.

John 15:4

"Remain united to me, and I will remain united to you. A branch cannot bear fruit by itself; it can only do so only if it remains in the vine. In the same way you cannot bear fruit unless you remain in me."

- ❖ Seek Jesus and live, be healed, receive prosperity, and be successful in every way forever and ever. He is your anchor, your support and nourishes you with his ability. Lay your life before him.

Be married to Jesus, be one with Jesus and be saved.

Psalm 98:4-9

Sing for joy to the LORD, all earth; praise him with songs and shouts of joy! Sing praises to the LORD! Play music on the harps! Blow trumpets and horns, and shout for joy to the LORD, our king. Roar, sea, and every creature in you; sing, earth, and all who live on you! Clap your hands, you rivers; you hills, sing together with joy before the LORD, because he comes he comes to rule the earth. He will rule the peoples of this world with justice and fairness.

- ❖ I Love you God, I love you Jesus; you are my love and you are holy and great, tremendous and miraculous. Your works astound me. I will forever revere you; I will forever commend you, adore you, honour you, and respect you because you are my healer, my comforter, my redeemer, my peace, my safety. You are my joy and happiness. You are the love of my heart. I love you God. I love you my King and Saviour.

Chapter 7

MY LORD AND MY SAVIOUR

John 14: 6

Jesus answered him, "I am the way, the truth, and the life; no one goes to the Father except by me."

- ❖ We have a personal relationship with Jesus as our mediator, it is God`s will that if we ask anything in the name of his Son Jesus he will grant us our request. Jesus is our confidence in asking from God. He is what is true for us, when we ask for healing, it is granted to us because Jesus conquered death on the cross for us. He is the gateway to salvation, he is upright, peace and justice, he is the one who support us when we are about to fall, he helps us, he leads us on to a good place full of goodness...he is one with the

Father and we are one in him...we are one in Christ and in all our ways. Because of the cross we are saved, we are not denied anything from God our Father in the name of Jesus.

John 14: 27

"Peace is what I leave with you; it is my own peace that I give you. I do not give it as the world does. Do not be worried and upset; do not be afraid."

- ❖ Jesus is our stronghold, he is the one who lifts us up high above and we receive God's love and mercy. When he comes into your life you feel his calmness, his assurance...his words of strength, he will speak gentle and tender words of comfort to your heart... when you feel things have gone wrong for you, he tells you... "It is well," this means everything will be fine with you; he will make your path clear and straight. You will never be afraid because nothing in this whole world is above him...he is the power that is above, he is your peace that pulls you through from the deepest end...he is our God who reigns and all rulers of this planet surrender and bow down to his command...therefore has authority to command disease and sickness to depart from your life! We have peace with Jesus......Isn't this what everybody wants and is looking for? Well, it is found in Jesus for God gave us his mercy through his Son Jesus and where there is mercy... there is peace and hope and life. It will never change, it's complete and sealed by the blood of Jesus, the blood of the lamb that was slaughtered for our sin...the lamb is Christ who took it all, he took away death and his peace in our lives is everlasting. Believe that God heals and takes you away from the path of death. Through Jesus Christ we are prepared to have life not death... Live and praise the Lord...pray for healing because God takes away all sadness and gives us surety of his sovereignty...he is able to give us life. Praise God all people!

John 15:9

"I love you just as the Father loves me; remain in my love."

- ❖ Jesus loves you ...yes, he does and he wants to continue having this loving life giving relationship with you. Tell him "I love you Jesus...be my Lord and Saviour." There is always a way with Jesus, he brings healing and peace and everlasting love... the world is a better place with him for in him there is the truth of the Father`s love...Our God.

John 16:20

"I am telling you the truth: you will cry and weep, but the world will be glad; you will be sad, but your sadness will be turned into gladness"

- ❖ Jesus died for us on the cross and took away all our sorrows; he died so that we may live a new life. That newness is given to us from God through the resurrection of Christ from death. We are conquerors through him and we live a complete life. Through him our brokenness is mended, our heart rejoice always, our darkness is turned into light because he broke the yoke that was oppressing us...the yoke of sin. We have God`s complete forgiveness from the origin of sin...the sin of Adam and Eve disobeying God. When we therefore continue to obey God we walk in the light of the Lord...we become one with him who redeemed us. We have his favour upon us. We are forever happy in Christ.

John 16:22

"Now you are sad but I will see you again, and your hearts will be filled with gladness, the kind of gladness that no one can take away from you. "

- ❖ Remember it is darkest before dawn, when you feel pressured and completely overwhelmed by the status quo of your existence, when darkness has enveloped you reach out to Jesus, he will answer you by bringing light into your life and the pressing situation will lose its grip on you… he is your personal saviour and always speak to him for he is near and will hear you. You are not lost but are found in Jesus Christ. Rejoice in him always.

John 16:24

"Until now you have not asked for anything in my name; ask and you will receive, so that your happiness may be complete."

- ❖ Because you are sad, because you are depressed, because you feel helpless and hopeless, because there is illness in your life, you have not known Jesus yet, he is not yet in you, you have not used the key to experience God`s outpouring in your life, you have not yet asked for the saving name of Jesus, make him your personal saviour who died for you on the cross so that you find your life, ask God the Father in heaven for anything you need in the name of Jesus and you will receive. Everything is made possible by God the Father through Jesus. All the pieces that have been shattered will come together like a puzzle built up and soon the whole picture will look beautiful and serene. Adore him and worship him, lay your life before him and he will renew you. Look for his heart that takes away all pain from you and gives you peace and joy and completeness. Let him make you whole...all you have to do is open your heart to him and ask from him. Love Jesus! Think Jesus! Sing Jesus!

John 16:27

"For the Father himself loves you. He loves you because you love me and have believed that I come from God. "

- ❖ Believe in Jesus as your saviour and be saved. The prayers that God answers are those presented to him through his Son. Acknowledging Jesus as God`s only Son brings honour to God because we are appreciating his act of mercy for us through him. We are appreciating him, we are saluting him, and we are lifting up his name when we accept Jesus as our only mediator to reach to our holy God. God died to self by sacrificing him for us. Our God is triune...we have the Father, Son and The Holy Spirit. All-Powerful, and Almighty to save, all-Redeeming Supreme God.

Jeremiah 31:20

"Israel you are my dearest son, the child I love best. Whenever I mention your name, I think of you with love. My heart goes out to you; I will be merciful."

- ❖ We are God`s children and we are close to his heart, he has us in him and we are blessed everyday to belong to such an awesome compassionate God. We will never be without comfort. His love for us is everlasting. When you lie down in sickness he will speak merciful words to you, he will raise you up and make you whole for you are the love of his heart....Rise up little one, rise your light has come and darkness is driven way...breathe... breath! God does not want to lose you...he needs your life for he is the One you praise...live and glorify his name. Hallelujah!

Isaiah 52:3

The Lord is saying to his people, "When you became slaves, no money was paid for you; in the same way nothing will be paid to set you free."

- ❖ When this sickness claimed your body you did not deserve it, you did not call upon this affliction and in the same way it came is the same way it will go, and it will go. There is a powerful way and that is the healing from God that comes through Jesus Christ. Jesus Brings healing, he turns that key that purifies you from the stronghold of disease and torture. The cross and his precious blood deliver us and God through his mercy pours life to us. Little one; be healed in the name of Jesus right now. God freely loves you and you do not need to pay the price for his love. In his love you are healed completely. Sing Hosanna to the Highest.

Chapter 8

THEY WILL CURSE, BUT MY GOD BLESSES.

Matthew 18:18

"And so I tell all of you: What you prohibit on earth will be prohibited in heaven, and what you permit on earth will be permitted in heaven."

- ❖ Break lose all curses that cling in your family life. Most people acclaim terminal illness as "acceptable" because it has claimed the lives of their relatives from generation to generation. This is not true, what happens to your grandfather, your uncles and cousins, brothers and sisters can be broken, there is no lineage of sickness, break it in the name of Jesus, reverse that power given to terminal illness as a stronghold in the name of Jesus and by the blood of Jesus claim your freedom from this hopelessness and oppression. Reverse it and ask God for healing and blessings for it is only God who hears and answers you. God is for us not against us, when we bind anything in the name of Jesus, God will permit, and when we ask for anything in the name of Jesus God will give. So right now in the name of Jesus we ask God our heavenly Father to break this spirit of infirmity from dominating and attacking us from our mother's bloodlines and from our father's bloodlines and we prohibit it to prosper in all generations to come in the name above everything. We ask God to cleanse and protect us with the blood of Jesus forever and ever and we prohibit this spirit of torment to enter our mortal bodies in the mighty name of Jesus. We pray that God will shower us with his blessings and protection and that we dwell in his presence every day of our lives. Be healed in the name of Jesus.

1John 4:2-3

This is how you will be able to know whether it is God's Spirit: anyone who acknowledges that Jesus Christ came as a human being has the Spirit who comes from God. But anyone who denies this about Jesus does not have the

Spirit from God. The spirit that he has is from the Enemy of Christ; you heard that it would come, and now it is here in the world already.

❖ When you plead the blood of Jesus on your life and when you call out his name and acknowledge that you are married to Jesus, then you will break all evil pressing you down. Evil refuse to speak out the name that took away condemnation and the name that is righteous and just. It cannot live inside you, It cannot face light, it cannot tolerate the person God used to reconcile mankind to himself, the person whom we are sanctified through, evil is then completely defeated and hence it will flee from you. Disease lose its hold on you, it becomes weak and subsides. It will never be a victor, it will not take its toll on you and in Jesus`s name you speak against it. It has no mastery on you. You are no longer preparing for death but you are getting ready to conquer and live a new life here on earth because your time to depart from the living is not yet now. Anything that belongs to God stays on you and that is your life, anything alien, anything causing discomfort and death will depart because the Spirit of the living God is upon you and it is a Spirit that helps you to overcome not to surrender to evil. It is a Spirit that gratifies in life not death;

it is life giving and our hope to live and to be anchored on its truthfulness and its love that will always be faithful. Declare allegiance to Christ and take his blood as a symbol of power and victory in your life and you will be safe because he is your Saviour and he lives in you. There is no harmony between the Spirit of truth that is God and the spirit of darkness. We know that God is eternal and will conquer for us eternally, we are free from fear and we have peace because we belong to life. Stop living in fear because of a certain particular disease that devoured your family. You were ignorant before of the power in the blood of Jesus. You are now a child of God and you were purchased by his blood and no evil can bring condemnation in your life. You are no longer a slave of this disease, you are free, and you are healed in Jesus.

I John 2:2

And Christ himself is the means, by which our sins are forgiven, and not our sins only, but also the sins of everyone.

- ❖ Jesus Christ came to save all; he came for our freedom and peace. He came to help us overcome the grip of Satan and all his weapons, we overcome in Christ because there is no more condemning, there is righteousness, there is uprightness, there is sustenance, there is mercy and compassion, there is gentleness, there is goodness and there is cleansing and love. Jesus is everything beautiful and graceful, there is purity and favour and we are victorious in him. We are made beautiful in Him.

I John 5:6-9

Jesus Christ is the one who came with the water of his baptism and the blood of his death. He came not only with the water, but with both the water and the blood. And the spirit himself testifies that this is true, because the Spirit is truth. There are three witnesses: the Spirit, the water and the blood; and all three have the same testimony. We believe man`s testimony; but God`s testimony is much stronger, and he has given this testimony about his Son.

- ❖ When we are baptised both by water and the Holy Spirit, we are completely given to God, we are children of God and the devil already knows we have chosen the supremacy of God whose Son died on the cross for our transgressions and whose blood was shed for us, whose side when pierced overflowed with blood and water a symbol of actual death of our sins because of human nature. We now live as his Spirit teaches us because he is the Spirit of truth, death and resurrection and the conquering of Satan and death itself. Declare the blood of Jesus upon your life and live to overcome, Satan cannot stand the truth about the cross, about God`s Son who obeyed him until death on the cross. He chokes upon the blood of Jesus and he loses all power because it is the blood that God glorified and justified us with as his children and forgave our sins which had allowed the devil power in our lives. Now the devil screams and runs away from us, everything that binds us flee with him and he is no more. So walk in the light of God. Walk with Jesus.

1Peter 1:17-21

You call him Father, when you pray to God, who judges all people by the same standard, according to what each one has done; so then, spend the rest of your lives here on earth in reverence for him. For you know what was paid to set you free from the worthless manner of life handed down by your ancestors. It was not something that can be destroyed, such as silver or Gold; it was the costly sacrifice of Christ, who was like a lamb without defect or flaw. He had been chosen by God before the creation of the world and was revealed in these last days for your sake. Through him you believe in God, who raised him from death and gave him glory; and so your faith and hope are fixed on God.

- ❖ We glorify God for giving us his only Son for salvation, peace and life. Knowing that we will forever overcome any strongholds in our lives; gives us peace and we feel safe and confident having the assurance of receiving healing from God through his Son Jesus Christ who conquered evil for us. We can in Jesus`s name and by his blood. Do not lose heart, do not be downcast, cheer up! Help is all around you for in Jesus there is a hedge of protection all around you. The evil One cannot prosper in his wickedness on your body, neither can he win your life; his clutches are all broken lose. There is sure hope for everything in Jesus Christ and we will continue to call upon his name. Our King and Saviour; our ruler who reigns in our lives forever and ever. We continue to seek his face, his mercy and healing.

Romans 9:1

I am speaking the truth; I belong to Christ and I do not lie. My conscience, ruled by the Holy Spirit, also assures me that I am not lying.

❖ God is forever faithful and truthful in his promises in our lives because he is the Spirit of truth in whom we have put our trust in. He heals us in his faithfulness and compassion. When he is with us we are at peace, we are not afraid of anything. We are not afraid of death.

Romans 6:6

And we know that our old being has been put to death with Christ on his cross, in order that the power of the sinful self might be destroyed, so that we should be no longer be the slaves of sin.

❖ The cross is a symbol of salvation....show the devil the cross and he will depart in a hurry, it overcomes him, it defeats him for it is light, it is life, it destroys darkness, it tears the devil`s ugly heart and he is lifeless, for on the cross Jesus died and on the cross the price for my sin was paid and the devil`s wicked schemes were made weak and useless. By the power of the cross evil becomes vain and bitter. It is completely sent to the bottomless pit, to despair and confinement and we are set free. We should rejoice for the saving power of the cross, we should rejoice for having the privilege to be reconciled with God through the blood of Jesus, we should sing new songs of freedom, songs of his mercy, songs that glorifies his name and his greatness for he touched us with his heart to love. He touched us and brought salvation in our lives.

1Peter 1:15-16

Instead, be holy in all that you do, just as God who called you is holy. The scripture says, "Be holy because I am holy."

- ❖ I am a child of God, and I do what Jesus do and I pray for his strength to live a good and obedient life free from evil desires and bad behaviour. I ask God to help me be a new person free from sin, I pray that the Lord Jesus Christ be my victor and bring his eternal victory in my life. I pray to be given the ability to lead a holy life, filled with his goodness and mercy, his splendour, his majestic ways and his grace. I pray for the power of the Holy Spirit to flow upon me and enable me to live as a child of light so that I conquer and parry off the advances of Satan in my life. I denounce him and ask the power of the Holy Spirit to protect me forever and ever in the name of Jesus.

Romans 6:12-14

Sin must no longer rule all your mortal bodies, so that you obey the desires of your natural self. Nor must you surrender any part of yourselves to sin to be used for wicked purposes. Instead give yourselves to God, as those who have been brought from death to life, and surrender your whole being to him to be used for righteous purposes. Sin must not be your master; for you do not live under Law but under God's grace.

- ❖ I surrender all to Jesus; I surrender my life, my soul, and all my ways to God my Father in heaven. I surrender to the light that outshines darkness, the light that conquers evil. I surrender to Jesus who died for me on the cross so that death may die and I receive life. I surrender my heart to my powerful and merciful God who has loved me and given me new life through Jesus Christ my Saviour and King. I surrender to God who rules and who is enthroned high above and to his Son who sits on his right hand and reigns forever in victory. I surrender to mercy, to compassion; to his beauty and his heart…I surrender to Jesus my healer.

1John 4:7-8

Let us love one another because love comes from God. Whoever loves is a child of God and knows God. Whoever does not love does not know God, for God is love.

- ❖ The devil does not know how to love but is after breaking you into pieces, he seeks to disrupt, to hinder progress, and he brings chaos and fear and captivity. You become afraid to move away from the fear instilled in your mind; you therefore remain in his stronghold. Therefore plead the blood of Jesus upon your life and loosen the stronghold of the devil`s schemes. The devil is full of lies and intimidation, he controls and rules your lives through lies, he breaks you through his falseness, he lures by pretending to be love…to be good, whilst he is not, he is quick to anger and condemn and punish…his vessels do not live long; for he destroys them, he cannot defend them because he is the one who leads them to darkness and away from what is good, he lets them succumb to death in despair and hopelessness, they are easy to welcome death rather than embrace life. The devil is heartless; he does not know what is good for he abhors God and goodness. The devil is a good pretender in order to win your souls for generations and generations, he lies to you that you are weak, you have genes for terminal diseases, that your lineage is not fit to live, you accept the lie and live in it until nothing good is left in families that worship him and encourage his ways by listening to his blunt life sentencing. Resist him, you will not be claimed by death in your early years. You will grow old and grey in the name of Jesus. We belong to God and therefore we are loved through Jesus Christ. Loving us was and is possible with God forever and ever. The devil lacks affection in all his ways; therefore, submit in all ways to God, and resist the devil, and he will leave you in many ways. God promises in Deutoromy 28:2 to bless us when we, "Obey the LORD your God…" Instead of curses we are blessed in every area of our lives… "he will bless our towns and our fields, we live in his safety, in good places full of his light, his joy and happiness, he will bless us with many children, many crops, and livestock….that he will bless us with his prosperity and wellness, he will pour out his abundance and success in our lives, the LORD will bless everything we do. He will fight our enemies and defeat them… whether disease, troubles, suffering and whether tormented or attacked, God will just defeat our enemies when they attack us, he says they will come at us in one direction but he will make them run from us in all directions. They will come from one direction but they will flee from you in seven directions…." and because God loves he will bless us. In Jesus Christ we are assured that we belong to him and there is no curse in our lives...they were taken and eradicated through the blood of Jesus and so we are placed high up above and not beneath. We live a life that is not borrowed but a life given to us through Jesus Christ... we have a rich spiritually, emotionally, physically, financially and socially fulfilled life, powered in Christ. Our families are blessed; there is neither sorrow nor death. We are able to face any challenges of life without fear of defeat for we know we will conquer in Christ and the power of our mighty God whom we worship and praise.

Romans 8:37-38

No, in all these things we have complete victory through him who loved us! For I am certain that nothing can separate us from his love: neither death nor life, neither angels nor other heavenly rulers or powers, neither the present nor the future, neither the world above nor the world below- there is nothing in all creation that will ever be able to separate us from the love of God which is ours through Christ Jesus our Lord.

1John 5:3-5

For our love for God means that we obey his commands. And his commands are not too hard for us, because every child of God is able to defeat the world. And we win the victory over the world by means of our faith. Who can defeat the world? Only the person who believes that Jesus is the Son of God.

Romans 8:28-30

We know that in all things God works for good with those who love him, those whom he has called according to his purpose. Those whom God had already chosen he also set apart to become like his Son, so that the Son will be the first among many brothers. And so those whom God set apart, he called; and those he called, he put right with himself, and he shared his glory with them.

Mark 12: 30

"Love the Lord your God with all your heart, with all your soul, with all your mind, and with all your strength."

- ❖ Surrender all that you are to God. Surrender to his will in your life and you will be safe. Do not be side tracked, do not waver; do not seek other ways beside your One and Only God. Obey him and live by his word alone. Lean on him in all ways, let his Spirit live in you. Walk a straight walk with Jesus then you will be victorious for he will shower you with many blessings, he will bless everything about you and everything you do and he will bless you with long life. You will live in his joy and happiness; you will be safe from the dangers of life and diseases. He will uplift you, he will carry you, and he will uphold you and fulfil you with the desires of your heart because you are operating in his will. He will continue to make you rich in his ways and he will open your eyes to greater things, things which you have never known; new things which only reside with him and only known to him, he will impart his wisdom, knowledge and understanding to you. He is supernatural God and we are right with God for he created us and the whole universe. Nothing can snatch you from the palms of God, nothing will attack you, no one will condemn nor curse you because you are covered in the shadow of his mighty wings, no stronghold will gain mastery in your life because you have chosen to belong to the ultimate power that makes you great and unattainable. God is your final help and solace. God gives life, and God is life, God is everlasting, self-existent, the Sovereign **I Am.** Holy, holy, holy is our God Almighty, majestic God, uncontainable, unattainable, undeniable authority, undisputable ability, guaranteed power for us, unchangeable God, truthful and loving God. "We adore you, we worship you because you are worthy of our praise. You are worthy to be our God."

Mark 11:25

"And when you stand and pray, forgive anything you may have against anyone, so that your Father will forgive the wrongs you have done."

- ❖ Come before God with clean hearts, the hearts filled with love for he was able to forgive us because of his love for us, hence we should also love and be able to forgive. Do not let your hearts be soiled by the world, shake it off by forgiving those who trespass against you, and ask the power of the Holy Spirit to help you. He is able to give you the will and ability to forgive with a free heart and separate yourself from that stronghold. Do not deny yourself a chance to a happier life by refusing to forgive those who have wronged you, walk away from the sin, it oppresses you and the person you cannot forgive. For God loved the world and he gave us his only Son Jesus to die on the cross for our transgressions, he forgave us by sacrificing his only Son to death. Therefore be holy because he is holy, forgive because you were forgiven in a greater way. Adopt a good heart, the heart of Christ, the heart of God and forgive whoever it is, be it your husband, your friend, your brother, sister, coworkers, fathers, mothers, your surrounding is full of people who are prone to error and who can hurt you, so be free from confinement to anger and forgive and seek God's love and mercy, and have a good personal relationship with him so that he gives you your requests freely because you would have allowed that freedom to come into your life. Be generous and God will be generous with you. Do away with the oppression of not forgiving, get rid of that selfishness and God will give you his abundance of mercy. Unforgiving hearts open windows for sin, when you cannot forgive you curse and curses are the result of an unforgiving heart, a heart that condemn and not bless. But our God is a forgiving God, he forgave hence through the person whom he used to forgive we break stronghold that oppress us; we break all curses because they came from an unforgiving hearts. Be good hearted not hard hearted for God's heart is good and merciful. When you forgive, your personal life is forgiven, your family stands forgiven with you, and your children prosper because of the presence of goodness in your heart.

Matthew 18:19-20

"And I tell you more: whenever two of you on earth agree about anything you pray for, it will be done for you by my Father in heaven. For where two or three come together in my name, I am there with them."

- ❖ Unity builds, when we cry out to God as prayer warriors, asking for his help, he will bring his healing speedily. If we join hands and in common agreement seeking his face and mercy in the name of our lord Jesus, he will help. The presence of the Holy Spirit enables us and guides us to what we ought to pray for, we are not alone and he is present in us…helping us to receive. He takes away fear and gives us confidence that whatever we ask from God in the name of Jesus his Only Son, we receive and that is a great promise. Because of this promise we are confidently assured to receive from our merciful and caring God who is devoted to us his children. We therefore constantly dedicate our prayers to him as our daily living bread. We are therefore surrendering him our burdens, and our requests will not go unanswered. "We love you Jesus, we love you Holy Spirit, our companion and helper, our teacher, our pillar, our strength, our foundation, and we are forever established in you." We receive complete healing through you, through your holiness and compassion; you considered us first.

1John 4:6

But we belong to God. Whoever knows God listens to us; whoever does not belong to God does not listen to us. This, then, is how we can tell the difference between the Spirit of truth and the spirit of error.

- ❖ Remember Satan and all his ways, and all his warriors...his demons are there to bring disruption in our lives, but we belong to power, we belong to light, and we belong to goodness in abundance, we belong to what is right and therefore everything wrong in our lives is put right in Jesus, through his blood and by his name we are saved, and the power of the Holy Spirit sets us in the right direction and we are forever healed in every area of our lives for we are prevented and protected from fatal errors of unrighteousness. We prefer to live powered by the Spirit of the living God, we read his word, we do what it says, we adore Jesus, we praise him we believe in his saving power for he is our God who is living and active in our lives, we live according to his precepts. The Holy Spirit is our hearts as our teacher, our counsel, who convict us and helps us to see right from wrong, he is our guide and we allow him to lead us because we need and seek his righteous ways and we obey what his word says and wait to receive from him as his children. We ask from him because he is a Father who richly blesses his children. We stand before him with confidence to receive help in love and mercy. Our needs are fulfilled.

Psalm 102:28

Our children will live in safety, and under your protection, their descendants will be secure.

- ❖ In Jesus`s name and blood I am comforted that my children will forever be free from the generations curses, and all strongholds of condemnation, my family is in the safety of his eternal presence, nothing can attack those who belong to Christ, when I am old and grey, I will depart from this world and go to heaven knowing that I have left my children in the peace of the Lord and that they walk by his ways and live in his safety and guidance for I have taught them to put God first. I have taught them to wait upon the Lord in all their ways and to ask for his favour and to worship him alone. I have taught them to put God forever before them for he touched me and healed me and gave me the blessing of a long life; a life that depend on him alone as my personal saviour and provider. My hearts is at peace knowing that; for generations and generations to come, my children will be blessed and walk in his light, filled by his inspiration and belonging to him alone. He is their good shepherd forever and ever. I thank God for this anointing. Blessed be to Jesus who died on the cross and who bled for my transgressions. "I love you my Father; I love you Jesus; and I love you Holy Spirit...triune God, maker of heaven and earth, powerful God, unattainable, uplifting, and ineffably sublime." He is a superior God. I am at peace, I am happy, for I have been made happy and strong, I am contented, I am fulfilled by his truthful and faithful ways. God is trustworthy and worthy of my life and my children and children's lives. And

I surrender them all to Jesus; I surrender their lives to Jesus.

Ephesians 6:10-13

Finally, build up your strength in union with the Lord and by means of his mighty power. Put on all the amour that God gives you, so that you will be able to stand up against the devil`s evil tricks. For we are not fighting against human beings but against the wicked spiritual forces in the heavenly world, the rulers, authorities, and cosmic powers of this dark age. So put on God`s armour now! Then when the evil day comes, you will be able to resist the enemy`s attacks; and after fighting to the end, you will still hold your ground.

- ❖ God is your defence on every area of your life, surround yourself with his presence by praying continually, reading his word, the bible, speak out his word and also do what it says you ought to do, let it live in you and live by it. Believe in Jesus as the Son of God who died for our sins, plead his saving blood upon your life. Ask for God`s guidance, his safety, his holiness, his uprightness and righteous ways to be imparted from him to you. Be true to God and yourself. And know that your strength comes from the divine fact that you were purchased by the blood of Jesus and you are saved from the result of sin and sin itself. You are free from condemnation and eternal despair for you belong to God and he is your shield, your victory, your helper, your hope, your rescuer from troubles, eternal God.

Hebrews 4:12-13

The word of God is alive and active, sharper than any double-edged sword. It cuts all the way through, to where all soul and spirit meet, to where joints and marrow come together. It judges the desires and thoughts of man's heart. There is nothing that can be hidden from God; everything in all creation is exposed and lies open before his eyes. And it is to him that we must all give an account of ourselves.

Ezekiel 18:4

The life of every person belongs to me, the life of the parent as well as that of the child. The person who sins is the one who will die.

❖ The things of the past are forever gone and will not affect us, neither the sins of our ancestors nor the weakness that afflicted them be passed on to our children. Every one of us has a personal relationship with Jesus Christ as a personal saviour. We are all before our God individually not overburdened by the sins of those who lived before us. Jesus took away all those burdens, all those curses are no longer oppressing us because the blood of the lamb cleansed us and we are free from this yoke of generational slavery. God through Jesus Christ crossed it all and all that debt is cancelled, pardoned, forgiven. We belong to God, and we are covered and sealed by the blood of Jesus and all curses are broken. We are free from condemnation, so tell the devil and his lies to, "back off, break lose, you have no place in my life." Nothing bad and evil runs in your family, it was all taken away and you are saved, reach out to God, do not let lies hold you prisoners, there is no hereditary weakness and generational disease in the Name of Jesus. He breaks them. God through Jesus's blood on the cross closed it all, he gave us power to stand, he put an end to this oppression. The cross made a huge difference in our lives, it is hope and safety, and it is healing and saving. "I love you Jesus....my Saviour, and my King, my everything my safety, my healer."

Chapter 9
HE HAS GIVEN ME LIFE.

John 10:27-30

"My sheep listen to my voice; I know them and they follow me. I give them eternal life and they shall never die. No one can snatch them away from me. What my Father has given me is greater than everything, and no one can snatch them away from the Father`s care The Father and I are one. "

- ❖ When you belong to God, you know his ways and nothing will lead you astray…you know God`s voice is warm and wooing, he speak guiding and glorifying words, he speak of peace, he speak of love, he speaks and declares that we will live even if we are on the verge of death…he speaks and brings life to us. We know his voice because when he speaks there is no threat but truth and promise, there a plea for what is right and the way to righteousness that is life giving. We are able to follow his commands because they are good and upright...the Lord`s ways builds and do not destroy, the lord`s voice does not waver, what he speaks remains and he will never change...his ways are as good, holy and righteous as he is...He is comforting and strengthening as he says words of wisdom and healing to us. God`s voice does not have contradiction and knows no defeat... he is forever powerful, anointing, refreshing and restoring. God`s voice is constructive, it does not cheat, it does not bait, it does not sound furious... it is forever kind and touches our hearts because it brings with it his love that we feel overwhelming and all merciful. There is warmth in everything God does and says. Satan can never sneak on us because we are quick to notice his blunt ways, his lies, his despair to ruin us...we know he is not our Good Shepherd because we were taught discernment. We are children of the light and we shun darkness. We are forever engraved in the palms of our God. Remember he gave us his Son to die for us, his body was pierced for our sins that could have brought everlasting death to us...but by his death on the cross we received life...we are healed because he was wounded for us. We are saved and we are forever under his care. Stand up and walk because you are healed. Praise God little flock. He loves you.

John 11:4

He said, "The final result of this illness will not be the death of Lazarus; this has happened in order to bring glory to God, and it will be the means by which the Son of God will receive glory."

- ❖ Do not be worried when you are ill…do not be disturbed that you are inflicted with this torturous pain, you will survive, and for this reason, sickness will speak of God`s truthful healing power and love for you. You shall be healed by the power of the Holy Spirit in the name of Jesus and the whole world will glorify God because of the good deeds he has done. When they glorify God because of you, you will also be lifted up in their praise and you will know and experience the joy of the Lord which forever gives you strength and purpose. Tell yourself, "The joy of the Lord is strength… the joy of the Lord brings life." You are not alone and you will not die but live to glorify his name. Praise the Lord!

Isaiah 61:11

As surely as seed sprout and grow, the Sovereign LORD will save his people. And all the nations will praise him.

- ❖ Just like the seed coming to life in growth so will you also rise from where you are put down. Keep fighting with determination to survive, hold on to life in Jesus`s Name. God wants you to grow and be old and wise. God is blessing you in your affliction, he is giving you life instead of death, grow…grow and be good…mount up on wings like an eagle and soar high above. Live a successful life filled with God`s care and presence and let the whole universe know that God is your only helper and shield, the one you trust because he gave you life when evil had brought death…God said "No" for you, death could not claim you. He rises in Power to save us.

John11:25-26

"I am the resurrection and the life. Whoever believes in me will live, even though he dies; and whoever lives and believes in me will never die. Do you believe this?"

- ❖ Lord you are the author and finisher of my life, when my good life you have given me in this world end when I am old and grey, I will still come to your eternity, death has no grip on me because you died for me and I am forever at peace. I will live long according to your promise and I love you Jesus! I live to prosper in your name Jesus!

John 12:46

"I have come into the world as light, so that everyone who believes in me should not remain in darkness."

- ❖ Remember...walk in the light...follow Jesus as the Lord and master of your life, follow his good ways...choose him not evil... call out to him in times of trouble and his light will shine upon you. God sacrificed his Son to atone for us. Death, trouble, guilty, sickness, suffering, self-condemnation, strife, anger, unfulfilled, fear, unhappiness, distraught, nervousness, unsure, undecided, failure, hopelessness, are fruits of darkness, they belong to the evil one. In Jesus we are saved from all troubles of life you can ever think of. Tell yourself you are set free from the clutches of the devil through the blood of Jesus.

You have given your life to God and nothing can overcome you. You are in his safe loving arms. You are under his wings and protected. All you have to do is to worship him and let him know you know he is there for you and will forever praise him. Make that effort even in your difficult situation and you will see his power which is wonder working.

John 14:19-20

In a little while the world will see me no more, but you will see me; and because I live, you will live. When that day comes, you will know that I am in my Father and that you are in me, just as I am in you. "

- ❖ We live by the power of the Holy Spirit in us... because he is the driving force in our lives we are led and guided to righteous ways. No child of God will continue to suffer or sin, the Holy Spirit in us helps us to be upright for it also convicts us when we are losing his upright ways. He draws us back to him. We fear God and when we fear God we know that his ways are forever upright and true, and you have to remain like him...in his uprightness. He is forever before you, teaching you his ways that bring everlasting love and everlasting life. In Jesus Christ we are completely sanctified. Come Holy Spirit...take control of our lives for you are worthy to receive our praise. You are beautiful Jesus...our Saviour and our King. You are the author of my life...you take me places which speaks of your presence to make me and the world whole again.

Psalm 80:3

Bring us back, Almighty God! Show us your mercy, and we will be saved!

- ❖ When I lose my faith, my trust, when the world has shaken me and makes me afraid , I ask for your help and guidance, I ask for you my saviour to tolerate my weakness and help me. When I face raging storms of life, in my weakness help me, in my flaws; have pity on me, in my sickness; heal me, in my lacking; provide for me, when I am restless; calm me, in my wilderness; show me the way and in my darkness, pour out your glory upon me for you are my saviour and redeeming God.

Psalm 84:11

The LORD is our protector and glorious king, blessing us with kindness and honour. He does not refuse any good thing to those who do what is right.

- ❖ God is always good all the time...he is perfect in all ways and make us feel valuable, we feel special when we receive his gift of life and love, we feel we are deserving and he sees it fit to bless us as our Father. With God we feel good, safe and healed. With God we feel motivated to be faithful, trusting and loyal because he is a truthful and life giving God. We live by his grace and peace and world becomes a better place for us because we know we can always run to him as our sanctuary...as our place of safety and he will forever protect us. God will never deny us his mercy, no matter what we have done in our previous life, when we come to know God, when we give him our lives, when we have changed our ways to become like Jesus...he will bless us in abundance...he will increase his blessings for us, we will overflow with his goodness. When healed, when saved, when protected, stand up and make an offer, give your life to him...to his ways and you will never lack anything and you will not face any more dangers for he will bless every area of your life with his love, peace and mercy. It's your way to a full potential life...always lean on him. Revere your God always and it will go well with you. The goodness of God is full of beauty, splendour, bright life and happiness.

Mark 9:25-26

"Deaf and dumb spirit," he said, "I order you to come out of the boy and never go into him again!" The spirit screamed, threw the boy into a bad fit, and he came out, and came out."

- ❖ Every obstacle oppressive in your life bows down to Jesus and obeys his command. Do not be afraid because you are being saved and freed from the chains of evil and death. He is above all and because he is your salvation, you will receive from the above all good things. Be healed in the highest name of Jesus. Walk!

Chapter 10

JESUS, YOU LOVE ME

Isaiah 42:6

"I, the LORD, have called you and given you power to see that justice is done on earth. Through you I will make a covenant with all peoples; through you I will bring light to the nations."

- ❖ We will not hung our heads in grief, shame and disgrace but we will rejoice in the Lord because of his blessings and saving hand. He takes pleasure in doing good things for us. He brings his light to us, his healing hands are on us and the yoke of sin, suffering and disease is forever broken. We are bathed in his saving light; the light that he has brought to our lives through Jesus Christ our Saviour….it is well with our souls.

Isaiah 42:7

"You will open the eyes of the blind and set free those who sit in dark prisons."

- ❖ Just give me your eyes so that I will see, bless me with your light that outshines my darkness, heal me with your saving power, break the yoke of suffering for me, you are the Lord of my life holy Jesus. I thank you God for giving me Jesus! He is my victor, my helper, my rock, my hiding place, my salvation and my peace, without him I am nothing; I am thrown into the bottomless pit of despair, enveloped in darkness. Come into my life forever and ever. Be my everlasting light.

John 15:9

"I love you just as the Father loves me; remain in my love."

- ❖ Thank you lord for your compassion; we are like a well-watered garden, beautiful and lacking nothing. Your light shines upon us and because of you, because of your love we are set free. There is no more pain and fear, for being loved is being healed, your love surrounds us and we have your joy and gladness. We are healed because you are with us.

Revelation 1:8

"I am the first, and the last," says the Lord God Almighty, who is, who was, and who is to come."

- ❖ We have one and only God who is forever watching over us, he is the only God who created the world in his goodness, who is everlasting in ruling, he pre-existed, he is self made, powerful and uncontested, undefeated and enthroned high above. Other than him there is no one else. He is our redeeming God, the love that sets us free from bondage. He is the supreme and majestic power we trust and anchor our hope in. Our truthful and faithful God; will not fail us or deny us his love. We completely depend upon him as our powerful saviour, holy and merciful. We praise him in holiness and for who is to us his children- our life giving God, our defender, the love of our hearts.

Acts 3:6

"Silver or Gold I do not have, but what I have I give to you. In the name of Jesus Christ of Nazareth, walk. "

- ❖ Be healed in the name of Jesus. Be completely healed in the name that is above every name!

John 14:13-14

"And I will do whatever you ask for in my name, so that the Father`s glory will be shown through the Son. If you ask me for anything in my name, I will do it."

- ❖ Lord, have mercy on me, heal me and set me free from bondage. I will praise you forever and ever. You are my life; you are all that I need, you are more than gold and silver to me, you more than the sun, moon and stars. You are my pure light. May your name be glorified; you are beautiful Jesus, my saviour and King. I pray for life because you are my able God.

Isaiah 42:16

"I will lead the blind by ways they have not known, along unfamiliar paths I will guide them; I will turn the darkness into light before them and make the rough places smooth. These are the things I will do; I will not forsake them."

- ❖ He will not fail you. His light is upon you and he is removing all that is causing you pain, he is taking away all hardship and setting you from the clutches of disease and sickness, tears of sorrows, he is removing you from the dark pit of despair and helplessness, he is creating a new beginning, a new life free of pain. Trust and believe, say loudly, "Jesus, I believe in you as my Saviour." Fill me with your presence and help me.

Ephesians 2:6-7

In our union with Christ Jesus he raised us up with him to rule with him in the heavenly world. He did this to demonstrate for all time to come the extraordinary greatness of his grace in the love he showed us in Christ Jesus.

- ❖ We are a sign of great power through Jesus; because we are saved and set free from evil. We rose with Jesus and therefore we conquer death. We are one with Christ and that is why we are healed. We belong to him; hence we belong to high power. We live in his miracles every day.

Romans 10:9

If you confess that Jesus is Lord and believe that God raised him from death, you will be saved.

- ❖ I believe in Jesus as the only begotten Son of God who died and rose from the cross so that I am set free from my sins and I believe he sets me free from the strongholds of life, from all that is pressing me down, I believe and trust he is my source of eternal life, my way to a holy and upright life, he is the truth of God`s existence in my life and through him I am pardoned from all my troubles and sins, I am healed, I have joy and happiness, I receive true mercy, through his victorious ways, I am give all that I ask for; I have confidence and peace in Christ, I am not afraid anymore, through him I know I am completely safe and will never be without help.

Romans 10:13

As the scripture says, "Everyone who calls out to the Lord for help will be saved."

- ❖ So help me Lord, save me, stretch out your hands and lift me up, my Saviour and comforter. Take away this pain and downhearted feeling, make me feel secure, help me to find my way out in this dark world. Help me to stand and I will stand, remove the feeling of shame, dejection and unhappiness, and change my world for me and create a better place for me, calm me and take away all fear of falling out.

Romans 16:20

And God our source of peace will soon crush Satan under your feet.

- ❖ Fight for me because I chose you. Send your angels of might into the camp of my enemy and confuse them and make me victorious. Smite the evil one. Lift me up to a higher standing. Let your power speak for me not against me. Bring me peace and not havoc for you are my safe place. Strengthen my trust in you by being my victor. Help me to be strong and to put out the fire of the evil one. Pull me through Lord.

Isaiah 30:19

You people who live in Jerusalem will not weep anymore. The LORD is compassionate, and when you cry to him for help, he will answer you.

- ❖ God is saying to you, "help is on the way, do not grieve, do not panic and do not be hopeless, you will be healed, there is no more sadness coming in your family but joy and relief. "

Romans 16:27

To the only God, who alone is all-wise, be glory through Jesus Christ forever! Amen.

- ❖ I thank you Lord for hearing my prayer and answering me and giving me words of comfort even though my world seems up-side-down. Thank you for being my God and for strengthening me. My Jehovah the greatest, my peace and my just God. My God who brings wellness in my life.

1 Corinthians 1:3

May God our Father and the Lord Jesus Christ give you grace and peace.

❖ You are my God who knows all my needs and I call out to you for help all my life...you alone. I pray that I live in your comfort and peace. You are my rest.

1Corinthians 8:3

But the person who loves God is known by him.

❖ May my God`s will be done in my life, let my will be like yours. May I live according to your divine ways...May I be healed of my undesirable ways. May I inherit from your rich kingdom? You are my God and my Rock and strength. Cover me in the shadow of your mighty wings. Protect me because I love you and I belong to you.

1Corinthians 2:16

As the scripture says, "Who knows the mind of the Lord? Who is able to give him advice?" We, however, have the mind of Christ.

- ❖ Put God first …he is a higher power, be humble always and learn to lean on him, for he, in his greatness, had mercy for us and he pardoned our sins by giving us his only begotten Son Jesus, to take away our shame by dying on the cross in humbleness and by his blood that was shed for us; we receive his Spirit of peace and power and strength and salvation….therefore having Christ as our Saviour give us peace in our hearts and rest in our minds. Nothing can overcome you. Are you suffering? Are you depressed? Are you angry? Are you dejected and upset? Are you discontented? Are you restless? Are you confused? Be at ease… receive Jesus Christ, receive his peace because he is saying to you, " Whatever is causing this pain, I am taking it away…and I give you my rest, my peace, because I am your Rock, I am your light, I will overcome for you, I remove this discomfort and it is now a thing of the past, I am filling you up with love and calmness, do not cry, do not lose heart for I am with you. Drink from me! I love you!" When we have Jesus we have a sound mind, a sound body and a sound relationship with him and our surrounding because he gives us guidance and support. Be comforted…you belong to a King who conquered death once and for all. He is forever conquering for us. God is the highest power in our lives and he gave us life through his Son. He is a merciful and healing

God. He healed us through Jesus Christ. You are beautiful Jesus.

John 4:13-14

Whoever drinks this water will be thirsty again, but whoever drinks the water that I will give him will never be thirsty again. The water that I will give him will become in him a spring which will provide him with life-giving water and give him eternal life.

- ❖ Jesus, you are my light, my guide, my teacher, my truth, my life. Help me to understand your word and live by it. Help me to seek all your good ways so that I live a long, healthy and good life. Help me to be righteous all the time. Take away the mess in my life and give me your cleanness. Spray me with your living waters and refresh and nourish me. Help me to grow and not die.

Chapter 11

JESUS TAKE CONTROL OF MY LIFE

1Corinthians 3:16-17

Surely you know that you are God`s temple and that God`s Spirit lives in you! So if anyone destroys God`s temple, God will destroy him. For God`s temple is holy, and you yourselves are his temple.

- ❖ God will forever fight for me and overcome the evil one for me. The devil has no room in my life, in my body, therefore I command the spirit of infirmity to leave in the name of Jesus…my body belongs to the Lord and I am not afraid of anything. He has full possession of my life. I am holy because I belong to a God who is holy and upright.

Psalm 46:5

God is in that city and it will never be destroyed; at early dawn he will come to its aid.

- ❖ I am strong in Jesus. The Spirit of the living God is upon me guiding me and protecting me; for he is my fortress. I will live and not die. God is enabling me to be victorious; his Spirit builds a wall of protection that shields me from the attack of the devil.

Romans 8:11

If the Spirit of God, who raised Jesus from death, lives in you, then he who raised Christ from death will also give life to your mortal bodies by the presence of his Spirit in you.

- ❖ You are not a slave of this disease; you are set free by the power of the Holy Spirit in the name of Jesus.

Romans 8:26-27

In the same way the Spirit also comes to help us, weak as we are. For we do not know how we ought to pray; the Spirit himself pleads with God for us in groans that words cannot express. And God, who sees into our hearts, knows what the thought of the Spirit is; because the Spirit pleads with God on behalf of his people and in accordance with his will.

- ❖ When I am weak then God is strong in me because his Spirit is in me and it helps me in my times of darkness and when I have lost all hope and am worn out by all my troubles. Reign upon my life Holy Spirit. Help me to breakthrough, may my supreme God who knows everything and is everywhere search my heart and help me; Spirit of God; lead me to the light because you are my light, take me under your wings. Untie the chains that bind me and bring me to victory. Sing for me, speak your words of healing to my life, and help me to stand up, help me to be strong again, take away my fear, take away my anguish, take away my vulnerability, make me feel secure and safe, guide and plead for me. Help me to live and praise you Holy Spirit. I long to live for you, Spirit of God, teach me your words and your ways. I Love you Lord, I love you Jesus.

John 17:25-26

"Righteous Father! The world does not know you, but I know you, and these know that you sent me. I made you

known to them, and I will continue to do so, in order that the love you have for me may be in them."

❖ Jesus is my Saviour and Redeemer, my knowledge and understanding. By his Spirit I live in complete joy and happiness that comes from the Father in heaven. He is amazing Christ.

John 16:13-15

When, however, the Spirit comes, who reveals the truth about God; he will lead you into all truth. He will not speak on his own authority, but he will speak of what he hears, and will tell you of things to come, he will give me glory, because he will take what I say and tell it to you. All that my Father has is mine; that is why I said that the Spirit will take what I give him and tell it to you.

❖ Shake yourself free from the chains that are binding you; believe and trust in his power; the Holy Spirit lives for us; it helps us through and the snares of the devil cannot hold its clutches on you. Feed yourself with the word of God and meditate upon what he is saying, then the Holy spirit will give you a sense of knowing, for the he is alert and he guides you always. Praise him for his many breakthroughs as you live your life, praise him for giving you the hope to live, praise him for his comforting presence. The Holy Spirit is that feeling you have that whatever you are doing is right, the decision you are making is the right one, he is that sure feeling in a mother that her child who is sick will live, and not succumb to death, it is a feeling that refuses to go away even if you are not accepting it. God will be writing your life for you. The good feeling stays, it lingers until it has fulfilled what it has been sent to do for you. There is no doubt about the saving power of the Holy Spirit. He is life giving, he shows us all truth and makes it come to be. When the Holy Spirit tells you that you will be fine...that will be the truth because he does not lie, he does not change, and will never fail you and that is the beauty of having him in you.

- ❖ He walks all the way with you, opening your eyes and revealing everything about your life and your surroundings. He is your success, your light, your teacher. He teaches you to be righteous; you will be able to discern between good and evil through the anointing of the Holy Spirit. Let the word of God into your hearts and let it speak to you, let it be firmly fixed within your heart, pray continuously and allow him to speak to you and help you to pull through the difficulties of life. He takes away the fear, the sadness, the anguish and bitterness. He heals you from that anger deep sitting within you by bringing it out to the surface and he helps you face it and deal with it until you are at peace. When you read the word of God, the word that the Spirit guides you into, it flows in you, it touches every part of your body, it touches your mind and sets you free from fear and the feeling of doom. Once it is in you; it constantly comes into your mouth, you speak it, you think through it; you start speaking God`s blessings in your life and the world around you. You speak what is good, you speak words of hope, you move away from despair and punishment. God himself will be teaching you and guiding you. He will comfort you through what you hear from his word. God is full of sympathy and his Spirit will never leave us in times of difficulties, he gives us strength and removes all weakness. His presence in your life is marked by his help, there is a definite turning point from your predicament, there is change, and hope that is fulfilled not denied. The Holy Spirit brings light to us and we are made complete. Drink to his words the words of hope and victory and be healed in the name Jesus.

Isaiah 61:1-3

The Spirit of the Sovereign LORD is on me, because the LORD has anointed me to preach good news to the poor. He has sent me to bind up the broken-hearted, to proclaim freedom for the captives and release from darkness for the prisoners, to proclaim the year of the Lord`s favour and the day of vengeance of our God, to comfort all who mourn, and provide for all who grieve in Zion- to bestow on them a crown of beauty instead of ashes, the oil of gladness instead of mourning, and a garment of praise instead of a spirit of despair. They will be called oaks of righteousness, a planting of the LORD for the display of his splendour.

John 7:37-38

"If anyone is thirsty, let him come to me and drink. Whoever believes in me, as the Scripture has said, streams of living water will flow from within him. "

- ❖ Believe in Jesus be healed. He is the good Spirit in you. He is God`s heart for us. He is our life giving water. Only through Jesus Christ our Saviour do we receive mercy from God. He is the way the truth and he is the life. Ask for healing in the name above every name, in the highest and wonderful name of Jesus.

Ephesians 4: 30-32

And do not make God`s Holy Spirit sad; for the Spirit is God`s mark of ownership on you, a guarantee that the Day will come when God will set you free. Get rid of all bitterness, passion and anger. No more shouting or insults, no more hateful feelings of any sort. Instead, be kind and tender-hearted to one another, and forgive one another, as God has forgiven you through Christ.

- ❖ God`s Spirit in us is not a spirit of chaos, disorder or turmoil, he is peace and always be at peace with him as well as your surroundings. Trust always in him and pray that he gives you strength to pull through and to hold firm to his word that is active in you. Surround yourself with his love and you will find rest. God is peace and love so always pray for his mercy which is the fruit of peace and love. Ask the Lord to help you be in harmony with everything. Do not let anything pull you down, close all windows that the devil might gain entry into your life. Submit completely to the saving power of God, this will put you at a confident and trusting relationship with God and then you will enable his healing flow to operate harmoniously in you, there is equilibrium of body, soul and mind. Our God is a God of balance, we are firmly footed in him and we will not fall sideways. He holds us and gives us steadiness and calmness because he is a dependable God and we trust that whatever we are asking from him he is working for us and bringing help, we will not be forsaken. He will never leave us with the desolate feeling that surrounds us when we are facing our weak moments. God forever tells us to be still and know that he is God, who is far above, supreme in all his ways and mighty.

Isaiah 60:1-2

Arise, Jerusalem, and shine like the sun; the glory of the LORD is shining on you! Other nations will be covered by darkness, but on you the light of the LORD will shine; the brightness of his presence will be with you. Nations will be drawn to your light, and kings to the dawning of your new day.

❖ If you believe in the light of the lord, if you believe in Jesus then you will be freed from darkness and be healed and saved from all troubles and suffering. Only believe and his light will shine upon you and you will walk and dance in jubilation. The whole world will see God`s favour and goodness upon those who trust and seek him and put him first as their Lord and Saviour. You will live a new life free from diseases and sorrow, God will forever protect you.

1John3:24

Whoever obeys God`s commands lives in union with God and God lives in union with him. And because of the Spirit that God has given us we know that God lives in union with us.

Revelation 3:20

Listen! I stand at the door and knock; if anyone hears my voice and opens the door, I will come into his house and eat with him, and he will eat with me.

Chapter 12

FOR, YOU HAVE LOVED ME!

1John 4:9

And God showed his love for us by sending his Son into the world, so that we might have life through him. This is what love is: it is not that we have loved God, but that he loved us and send his Son to be the means by which our sins are forgiven.

1Corinthians 13:2

I may have the gift of inspired preaching; I may have all knowledge and understand all secrets; I may have all the faith needed to move mountains-but if I have no love, I am nothing.

I Corinthians 13:4-8

Love is patient and kind; it is not jealous or conceited or proud; love is not ill-mannered or selfish or irritable; love does not keep a record of wrongs; love is not happy with evil, but is happy with the truth. Love never gives up; and its faith, hope, and patience never fail. Love is eternal.

John 5:1-9

Jesus went to Jerusalem for a religious festival. Near the Sheep Gate in Jerusalem there is a pool with five porches; in Hebrew it is called Bethzatha. A large crowd of sick people were laying in the porches- the blind, the lame- and the paralysed. A man was there who had been ill for thirty-eight years. Jesus saw him lying there, and he knew that the man had been ill for such a long time; so he asked him, "Do you want to get well?" The sick man answered, "Sir, I have no one here to put me in the pool when the water is stirred up; while I am trying to get in, somebody else gets there first." Jesus said to him, "Get up, pick up your mat, and walk." Immediately the man got well; he picked up his mat and started walking.

John 15:7

"*If you remain in me and my words remain in you, then you will ask for anything you wish, and you shall have it.* ``

John 15:13

"The greatest love a person can have for his friends is to give his life for them. "

I John 3:14

We know that we have left death and come into life; we know it because we love our brothers. Whoever does not love is still under the power of death.

- ❖ When we extent our hearts to those suffering and ill, and surrender our lives to help them receive healing and be well again; then we know we have Christ in us, we know we belong to the light that is the love for other people. Pray for your friends, your neighbours, your siblings… pray for the world to be healed, touch somebody and God will touch you. God also uses vessels for his glory and honour; that is to bring his saving power into the world. God also pours it upon you when you reach out to him…without ever bringing anyone to you. He can do anything by himself, but when he uses you he is inviting you to have a share of His kingdom, to be a contributing person, with purpose and so he looks into your heart and when he sees potential compassion he blesses you in whatever you do, and put you in places where you are able to make sound and glorifying decisions for his purpose and Kingdom. It is very essential to be a loving and kind person... it opens God`s supreme ways for you. All you do is to open your heart to his call. God speaks in different ways. Even in illness you can be called to help others with the same help you received from him. Through compassion you understand the pain they are going through and will offer yourself to help them. When you have hate... then you are as bad as a murderer because you have no love and do not belong to eternal life, you do not belong to light but darkness. Love God and live.

Psalm 59-17

I will praise you, my defender. My refuge is God, the God who loves me.

1 John 5:20

We know that the Son of God has come and has given us understanding, so that we know the true God. We live in union with the true God- in union with his Son Jesus Christ. This is the true God, and this is eternal life.

Psalm 60:5

Save us by your might; answer our prayer so that the people you love may be rescued.

Psalm 62: 5-7

I depend on God alone; I put my hope in him. He alone protects and saves me; he is my defender, and I shall never be defeated. My salvation and honour depend on God; he is my strong protector; he is my shelter. Trust in God at all times, my people. Tell him all your troubles, for he is our refuge.

Isaiah 54:10

"The mountains and hills may crumble, but my love for you will never end; I will keep for ever my promise of peace." So says the LORD who loves you.

Psalm 63:6-8

As I lie in bed, I remember you; all night long I think of you, because you have been my help. In the shadow of your wings I sing for joy. I cling to you, and your hand keeps me safe.

Psalm 63:3-4

Your constant love is better than life itself, and so I will praise you. I will give you thanks as long as I live; I will raise my hands to you in prayer.

Ephesians 2:8-10

For it is by God`s grace that you have been saved through faith. It is not the result of your own efforts, but God`s gift, so that no one can boast about it. God has made us what we are, and in our union with Christ Jesus he has created us for a life of good deeds, which he has already prepared for us to do.

Psalm 44:3

Your people did not conquer the land with their swords; they did not win it by their own power; it was by your power and your strength, by the assurance of your presence, which showed that you loved them.

❖ Only by God`s Spirit, I will overcome.

1John4:18

There is no fear in love; perfect love drive out all fear. So then, love has not been made perfect in anyone who is afraid, because fear *has to do with punishment.*

1 John 4:19

We love because God first loved us.

Psalm103:11-14

As high as the sky is above the earth, so great is his love for those who honour him. As far as the east is from the west, so far does he remove our sins from us. As kind as a father is to his children, so kind is the LORD to those who honour him. He knows what we are made of; he remembers that we are dust.

Chapter 13

MY GOD, LIFT ME UP

Psalm 61:2

In despair and far from home I call to you! Take me to a safe refuge, for you are my protector, my strong defence against my enemies.

Psalm 63:1

O God, you are my God, and I long for you; like a dry, worn-out, and waterless land, my soul is thirsty for you.

Psalm 55:16-17

But I call to the LORD for help, and he will save me. Morning, noon and night my complaints and groans go up to him and he will hear my voice. He will bring me safely back from the battles that I fight.

- ❖ Do not give up on your prayers to God...make it part of your life, your daily bread, in sickness and in health. You will forever have victory over all strongholds that torment you.

Psalm 41:3

The LORD will help them when they are sick and will restore them to health.

Psalm107:18-21

They couldn`t stand the sight of food and were close to death. Then in their trouble they called to the LORD, and he saved them from their distress. He healed them with his command and saved them from the grave. They must thank the LORD for his constant love, for the wonderful things he did for them.

Psalm 41:4

I said, "I have sinned against you, LORD; be merciful to me and heal me."

Psalm 41:8, 10, 12

They say, "He is fatally ill; he will never leave his bed again."......Be merciful to me, LORD, and restore my health...... You will help me, because I do what is right; you will keep me in your presence forever!

Psalm 88: 8, 9

I am confined and cannot escape; my eyes are dim with grief. I call to you, O LORD, everyday; I spread out my hands to you.

Psalm 43:3

Send your light and your truth; may they lead me and bring back to Zion, your sacred hill, and to your temple where you live.

Isaiah 43:1-3

"Do not be afraid- I will save you. I have called you by name- you are mine. When you pass through deep waters, I will be with you; your troubles will not overwhelm you. When you pass through fire, you will not be burnt; the hard

trials that come will not hurt you. For I am the LORD your God, the holy God of Israel, who saves you."

Psalm107:14

He brought them out of their gloom and darkness and broke their chains in pieces.

Psalm 106:4

Remember me LORD, when you help your people; include me when you save them.

Chapter 14

HIS WONDERFUL PEACE HEALS

Psalm 20:1-5

May the LORD answer you when you are in distress; may the name of the God of Jacob protect you. May he send you help from the sanctuary and grant you support from Zion. May he remember all your sacrifices and accept your burnt offerings. May he give you the desire of your heart and make all your plans succeed. We will shout for joy when you are victorious and will lift up our banners in the name of our God. May the LORD grant all your requests.

- ❖ Our God works for us not against us, he wants to bless us so much and give us his good grace, therefore we ask from him all the good things in life, we ask to be saved, to be successful, to be prosperous in all ways, to break through in everything good that we set our hearts to do, we also want to reach out to him extending our gratitude by giving him offerings for his kingdom and receive more from him, and this is our way of thanking God for keeping us safe...we want to bless the world through him. We want our lives to be a joyful song because we are children of a holy, powerful, merciful and life-giving God and we are calling for a peaceful relationship him.

Philippians 4:6-7

Don't worry about anything, but in all your prayers ask God for what you need, always asking him with a thankful heart. And God's peace, which is far beyond human understanding, will keep your hearts and mind safe in union with Christ Jesus.

- ❖ Do not just cry about your troubles, do not let yourself fall, neither should you take God for granted by giving him a silent treatment, say out everything to him believing and trusting he will change your situation. Pour out those words to him, do not bottle your pain and worry for it will overcome you, tell it as it is to the Lord in your prayer. Keep saying heal me Lord, and save me

Lord, because he is your peace bringing God, he is the therapy you need, and you will be revived. He is always with you and when everything else fails, God will never fail you...he is available and able. You have his peace.

Philippians 4:4-6

Rejoice in the Lord always. I will say it again: Rejoice. Let your gentleness be evident to all. The Lord is near.

- ❖ No matter how far you seem from the Lord, no matter how difficult your trials and tribulations are, submit to the joy of the Lord. Always be happy and stay positive and believe that you will overcome in his joy and he will bring peace according to his promise in your life, he created you so that you live a long life blessed and with an overflow of everything that comes from him as your everlasting God. Be happy do not be afraid, God is helping you in the name of Jesus. When you believe, anything you believe in will happen. God promises our mothers in, Deuteronomy 28:4 saying to them, "The fruits of your womb will be blessed." He will bless the living not those in the grave, therefore he wants you to live and the devil is defeated, Satan's curse of this sickness and trouble is wiped out, and is completely removed from your body and as you rest on your bed praise God because you are living and breathing. Say I will not die because I have a saviour and his name is Jesus...Rejoice because he is your miracle worker, your healer.

Philippians 4:8-9

Finally, brothers, whatever is true, whatever is noble, whatever is right, whatever is pure, whatever is lovely, whatever is admirable- if anything is excellent or praiseworthy- think about such things. Whatever you have learned or received or heard from me, or seen in me-put into practice. And the God of peace will be with you.

❖ Do not dwell on your problem, do not listen to that illness and be tumbled down and under by it, think positive things, think about the goodness of God, see him working for you and in you, dwell on his love, on his word, and stay optimistic, tell him you praise him because he is your helper and that you are not being denied. You are not in denial but in God`s favour and he is healing you. You know exactly that he will do it. So be glad and rejoice, be prepared to live and not die. Remember God gave us his only Son Jesus to die for us, Philippians 2:9-11*"Therefore God exalted him to the highest place and gave him the name that is above every name, that at the name of Jesus every knee should bow, in heaven and on earth and under the earth, and every tongue confess that Jesus Christ is Lord."* This is your powerful healer and saviour, nothing is impossible in his name. Nothing refuses to bow down, disease is succumbed and Jesus is our light, he set us free from prisons of life troubles. You are not a prisoner of terminal illness...you are victorious in Jesus. Nothing can challenge the blood of Jesus over your life. It is impossible for the disease to linger in your body because it will just be washed away with his blood like the way soap removes dirt under the shower. It is completely eradicated and your body will feel clean and remain with the fragrance of the blood which the devil hates because of its sweet aroma. The aroma of life. The devil hates peace and life, God loves peace and life, and he brings order to your life. Sickness brings chaos and sorrows; but we say to the devil," it is done, it is finished, back off!" Devil, go in the name of Jesus and never come back. And so it is done! When you have Jesus; troubles, difficulties and sickness is something which you should never be afraid of, it is weak and powerless, vain and in despair, it is completely hopeless and you are stronger. So fear not, little star. Rise and shine. Amen.

Colossians 1:3

We always give thanks to God, the Father of our Lord Jesus, when we pray for you.

- ❖ We praise him for his great love and mercy and goodness in your life. He is an awesome God. I love you God Almighty be with me forever and ever.

Colossians1:15-20

Christ is the visible likeness of the invisible God. He is the fist- born Son, superior to all created things. For through him God created everything in heaven and on earth, the seen and the unseen things, including spiritual powers, lords, rulers, and authorities. God created the whole universe through him and for him. Christ existed before all things, and in union with him all things have their proper place. He is the head of his body, the church; He is the source of the body`s life. He is the first- born Son, who was raised from death, in order that he alone might have the first place in all things. For it was God`s decision that the Son has in himself the full nature of God. Through the Son, then God decided *to bring the whole universe to himself. God made peace through his Son`s death on the cross and so brought back to himself all things, both on earth and in heaven.*

- ❖ Jesus Christ has the divine power to heal you and save you. He is of the above, enthroned up high with God the Father. Do not stager, be stable and be confident that it will soon come to pass and God`s healing power is true and it will be! How glorious and powerful is our God will soon be revealed in your healing. He is able to restore you to a sound, healthy body. Now it is easy to see God…his works for our lives are all perfect and renewing. In Jesus you will not die but live! We were bought by his life giving blood….when you speak the blood of Jesus and plead it upon your life, the devil flees, darkness departs and you are filled with the glow of the Lord. God is saying to you … "You are mine." Say to him, "I am all yours in completeness." Always remember, "Everything holds together for you in Jesus Christ." Jesus is, my Saviour, my Christ.

Colossians1:23

You must, of course, continue faithful on a firm and sure foundation, and must not allow yourself to be shaken from the hope you gained when you heard the gospel.

- ❖ Hold on to the love of God; resist all evil thoughts, chose life not death. Surrender then; to Jesus Christ.

Colossians 4:2

Be persistent in prayer, and keep alert as you pray, giving thanks to God.

- ❖ Prayer is very important for you, it moves mountains and any obstacles in your path, it enables the Spirit of the living God to operate for you. Remember God always answer prayers. Never give up, do not be discouraged by anything for God works in ways you cannot see because he is mighty and supreme. He will never abandon you. Be strong in prayer, it's your warm and safe place, and it draws you closer to God.

1Timothy2:5-6

For there is one God, and there is one who brings God and mankind together, the man Christ Jesus, who gave himself to redeem all mankind. That was the proof that at the right time God wants everyone to be saved.

❖ Only God can save us through reconciliation he brought us through the blood of Jesus. From there we receive mercy in abundance; nothing is denied to us by God when we ask him for anything in the name of his Son Jesus Christ. The best thing we have in our lives is the saving power in the blood of Jesus. It is a living testimony in our lives because the burden of condemnation and death was lifted from us. Our peace is firmly rooted in Christ and the love of God.

Chapter 15
MY REDEEMER LIVES

Galatians1:3-5

May God our Father and the Lord Jesus Christ give you grace and peace. In order to set us free from this present evil age, Christ gave himself for our sins, in obedience to the will of our God and Father. To God be the glory forever and ever! Amen.

Psalm 49:7-9

A person can never redeem himself; he cannot pay God the price of his life, because the payment for human life is too great. What he could pay is never enough to keep him from the grave, to let him live forever.

❖ By his mercy, God was able to redeem us through his son Jesus and hence brought victory into our lives. He already suffered for us on the cross and we cannot suffer again, declare this and live. He can and will save you. By his obedience to God`s will in him for us, Jesus Christ did not hesitate to die for us, he was in turn compassionate and laid down his own life for us knowing he will rise again for our eternity. This is God`s gift of his love for us. Being able to love is a holy gift that removes evil; it kills the devil and his schemes. We are only afflicted on flesh but we are strong in spirit because the Spirit of the Lord is in us. When the spirit is strong and willing...then there is life for it will be clinging to life. Hold on to Jesus and win your battle. Have the strong will to live...be determined and know that the Spirit of God that empowers you is strong and powerful. God has no boundaries, nothing can stop him, no words and action can defeat God. He is the undefeated, immortal and eternal God. King of kings, Lord of creation. Our only Saviour.

Psalm116:8-11

The LORD saved me from death; he stopped my tears and kept me from defeat. And so I walk in the presence of the

LORD in the world of the living. I kept on believing, even when I said, "I am completely crushed," even when I was afraid and said, "No one can be trusted."

- ❖ Praise the Lord for his help and love for you, praise him for bringing you joy, make offerings for being saved from death, touch other people with another kind of help, make the Lord happy and give him your heart. Let him lead you forever in your life for he gave you the strength to keep you hoping in spite of your deep trouble and hopelessness. Do not forget God`s love and compassion, be grateful to him and he will bless you with more in the new life he has given you. When you are healed feel the pity he had for you and say; Psalm116:12-14 "What can I offer the LORD for all his goodness to me? I will bring a wine offering to the LORD, to thank him for saving me. In the assembly of all his people I will give him what I have promised." This is your peace and it glorifies God and he will forever protect you and reward you, for you know how to please him.

Job 19:25-27

I know that my redeemer lives, and that in the end he will stand upon the earth. And after my skin has been destroyed, yet in my flesh I will see God; I myself will see him with my own eyes- I and not another. How my heart yearns within me!

- ❖ God is the only one who has the power to defend us in a permanent and undoubtedly way. In many cases our trials are so severe and discouraging, it is all dark, no one seems to know how else to help, we all run out of ideas and ways, whatever we try to change the situation is only a cry of desperation that worsens the situation and result in chaos and disorder, so many times the end is loss of lives. But there is only one way...that way is Jesus, whom our God, who is everlasting, gave to us so that we have eternal life, a life ease of troubles, we are completely healed by his mercy. John 10:10 Jesus said, "I have come in order that you might have life- life in all its fullness." This is our hope, our anticipation and our yearning. With Jesus we know we have already won the battle and we speak of it and make it known to our tormentor that his affliction will not lead to death but restoration. Look direct into your tormentor's face and break his attacking advance by declaring that God lives for you and will help you, and that you will be above not beneath because you belong to a higher and mightier power. This would cause your stronghold to be subdued and you become victorious for in no time it loses its menace on you, it will put its weapons against your life down because the Power of the living God will overcome for you. You cannot fight your battle alone; God is your helper and through the blood of Jesus you win... you are not a looser, neither are you vain. All you have to do is to lean on him.

John 6:51

"I am the living bread that came down from heaven. If anyone eats this bread, he will live forever. The bread that I will give him is my flesh, which I give so that the world may live.``

Psalm 18:9-14

He tore the sky apart and come down with a dark cloud under his feet. He flew swiftly on a winged creature; he travelled on the wings of the wind. He covered himself with darkness; thick clouds, full of water, surrounded him. Hailstorm and flashes of fire came from the lightning before him and broke through the dark clouds. Then the Lord thundered from the sky; and the voice of the Most High was heard. He shot his arrows and scattered his enemies; with flashes of lightening he sent them running.

Psalm 16:9-10

And so I am thankful and glad, and I feel completely secure, because you protect me from the power of death, and the one you love you will not abandon to the world of the dead.

Psalm 16:11

You will show me the paths that lead to life; your presence fills me with joy and brings me pleasure forever.

Psalm116:1-4

I love the LORD because he hears me; he listens to my prayers. He listens to me every time I call to him. The danger of death was all around me; the horrors of the grave closed in on me; I was filled with fear and anxiety. Then I called to the LORD, "I beg you, LORD, save me!"

- ❖ The love of God eradicates fear and anxiety, it is crushed...fear belongs to evil and it is a weapon used by the devil to disable our faith and firmness.

Stand on solid ground in Jesus Christ. Be as solid as a rock because you are created in the likeness of your Rock; Jesus! You live, you rise, you survive, you thrive, and you are solid.

Psalm118:5-6

In my distress I called out to the LORD; he answered me and set me free. The LORD is with me, I will not be afraid; what can anyone do to me?

- ❖ God is our everlasting protection. His love for all is eternal and majestic, supreme in all ways.

Psalm 118:17

I will not die; instead I will live and proclaim what the LORD has done.

- ❖ You are our glorious God; we give you honour and praise, for you are our saviour and Redeemer. You are our hiding place.

Psalm 116:5-7

The LORD is merciful and good; our God is compassionate. The LORD protects the helpless; when I was in danger, he saved me. Be confident, my heart because the LORD has been good to me.

- ❖ Nothing compares to our God. He did a matchless gesture of love for us by sacrificing his only Son for our transgression and through Jesus Christ we receive life in this world as well as the world of the dead for we rose with him from the cross. We are always in his light.

Colossians 3:1

You have been raised to life with Christ, so set your hearts on the things that are in heaven, where Christ sits on his throne at the right hand of God.

- ❖ Let's kneel down and worship the Lord in his highness, let's praise him with life giving songs, songs of his greatness, songs of joy, for he is our beloved God, our King of kings and Lord of lords. Everything is beneath him, he is our strong tower of refuge, he is the, **I am**, that was, and that is, and that will forever be in our lives. He defeated for us before, he will defeat for us now and forever...we will never be afraid for we have Jesus as the Lord of our lives, our Redeemer who lives forever and ever. Come Jesus, reign in our lives! Forever save us! Forever protect us! Forever help us! Forever comfort us! Amen.

Revelation 21:3-4

"Now God`s home is with mankind! He will live with them, and they shall be his people. God himself will be with them, and he will be their God. He will wipe away all tears from their eyes. There will be no more death, no more grief or crying or pain. The old things have disappeared."

- ❖ Thank you Holy Spirit for living in us and with us, helping us and upholding us. You are the power that carries us.

Revelation 21:6

And he said, "It is done! I am the first and the last, the beginning and the end. To anyone who is thirsty I will give the right to drink from the spring of water of life without paying for it. Whoever wins the victory will receive this from me: I will be his God, and he will be my son."

Revelation 22:17

The Spirit and the Bride say, "Come!" Everyone who hears this must also say, "Come!" Come, whoever is thirsty, accept the water of life as a gift, whoever wants it.

- ❖ There is room for us in Christ, he is open armed to receive us when we call for his presence and love in our lives.

Revelation 22:20

"Yes indeed! I am coming I am coming soon!" So be it. Come, Lord Jesus!

Chapter 16
I LOVE YOU JESUS

2 Corinthians 12:9

But his answer was: "My grace is all you need, for my power is strongest when you are weak."

- ❖ When we have lost all hope, when we are empty, when we are troubled, when we are succumbing to death in sickness then he rises in power to save us. He heals us, he rescues us, and he restores and revives us. God is amazing and abounding in love. He is the strength that we need. He is life.

John14: 21

"Whoever accepts my commandments and obeys them is the one who loves me. My Father will love whoever loves me; I too will love him and reveal myself to him."

- ❖ When you love Jesus you also love God because they are one and the same, we have a triune God who is: Father, Son and the Holy Spirit. Triune God is all-powerful three in one.

2 Corinthians 1:3-5

Let us give thanks to the God and Father of our Lord Jesus Christ, the merciful Father, the God from whom all help comes. He helps us in all our troubles, so that we are able to help others who have all kinds of troubles, using the same help that we ourselves received from God. Just as we have a share in Christ`s many sufferings, so also through Christ we share in God`s great help.

1John 5:18

We know that no child of God keeps on sinning, for the Son of God keeps him safe, and the Evil One cannot harm him.

Psalm16:8

I am always aware of the LORD`s presence; he is near and nothing can shake me.

Psalm 16:2

I say to the LORD, "You are my Lord; all the good things I have come from you."

Psalm 34:18

The LORD is near to those who are discouraged; he saves those who have lost all hope.

Chapter 17

YOU CAME FOR ME!

Isaiah 35:1-10

The desert will rejoice, the flowers will blossom in the wilderness.

The desert will sing and shout for joy; it will be as beautiful as the Lebanon Mountains and as fertile as the fields of Carmel and Sharon.

Everyone will see the LORD`s splendour, see his greatness and power.

Give strength to hands that are tired and to knees that tremble with weakness.

Tell everyone who is discouraged, "Be strong and don`t be afraid!

God is coming to your rescue, coming to punish your enemies``

The blind will be able to see, and the deaf will hear.

The lame will leap and dance, and those who cannot speak will shout for joy.

Streams of water will flow through the desert; the burning sand will become a lake, and dry land will be filled with springs.

Where jackals used to live, marsh grass and reeds will grow.

There will be a highway there, called "The road to Holiness``

No sinner will travel that road; no fools will mislead those who follow it.

No lions will be there; no fierce animals will pass that way.

Those whom the LORD has rescued will travel home by that road.

They will reach Jerusalem with gladness, singing and shouting for joy.

They will be happy for ever, forever free from sorrow and grief.

- ❖ Jesus came for us to receive salvation, hope, beauty in every area of our lives; he came so that we receive healing and good life. We have security and peace through him. The love of God is manifested. He came to rescue us from the evil one, from the scares of life, from all dangers, injustice and to remove disgrace smeared upon us, he came to lead us to righteousness that brings joy to life, he came to help us lead our lives free of sin. Jesus Christ was sacrificed for our eternal joy and happiness. Be healed in his name. May God Almighty touch every area of your life by his love and mercy and bring complete healing in your life. God judges those who condemn us and those who fight us, he will discipline. There is no more darkness but light and bright life, every vile intention from the enemy is quickly exposed and destroyed. There is safety in Christ...we shall not be afraid of anything, he is our victory, and victimisation is removed. Believe you are not a victim of a diseased life but you have peace and comfort. He is our strength; he is our God of retribution who will forever save us. We therefore live in laughter and happiness. Joy, joy, joy...we receive eternally and we will sing Hosanna to the Highest and Almighty Sovereign triumph God.

Revelation 22:5

There shall be no more night, and they will not need lamps or sunlight, because the Lord will be their light, and they will rule as kings forever and ever.

- ❖ God is the source of our joy, honour and pride; he makes us powerful as kings in our lives. We should always fear and respect God. He brought eternal love and life to us. As children of God… we have all his goodness and splendour, nothing should sneak on you because you belong to the visible light that is Jesus Christ our saviour.

Acts 16:31

"Believe in the Lord Jesus, and you will be saved- you and your family.``

- ❖ Jesus you are the light of my life, my Saviour and my Lord! You are my King, my glory, my salvation, my trust and my love. You are my everlasting light and my gateway to safety. Help me in all my ways, be the center of my life, be the light of my feet, be my complete vision. Take away all my darkness and bring your everlasting peace and sound life.

John 14:6-7

Jesus answered him, "I am the way, the truth, and the life; no one goes to the Father except by me. Now that you have known me, `` he said to them, "you will know my Father also, and from now on you do know him and you have seen him. ``

- ❖ I believe in you triune God, Father, Son and Holy Spirit. All- Powerful, All-merciful, all-loving, All-wise and all-knowing, All-peaceful, All-saving... my great God. I am empowered by you and I am victorious in you and I am healed by you. Help my soul most powerful God from all my sins. Pour out your tender mercies upon me and bring comfort to my life.

Isaiah 9:6-7

A child is born to us! A son is given to us! And he will be our ruler. He will be called, "Wonderful Counsellor," "Mighty God," "Eternal father," "Prince of Peace." His royal power will continue to grow; his kingdom will always be at peace. He will rule as King David`s successor basing his power on right and justice, from now until the end of time.

- ❖ Come Lord Jesus into my Life! My King, my strength, my banner, my support, my guide, my rest, my justice, my power, my everything. I love you...my Messiah, the promised Saviour, my salvation. Holy Spirit, My God.

Revelation 22:14

Happy are those who wash their robes clean and so have the fruit from the tree of life and go through the gates into the city.

- ❖ Jesus help me to be holy; teach me your righteous ways and give me your uprightness for you are the Lord of my life. You are my saviour and my restorer, my great power, my God who heals all my faults, shower me with your cleansing light and let your light fall upon me forever and ever, most redeeming God.

Revelation 22:12-13

"Listen!" Says Jesus. "I am coming soon! I will bring my rewards with me, to give each one according to what he

has done. I am the first and the last, the beginning and the end."

- ❖ There is only one personal saviour and his name is Jesus, apart from him; whose blood was shed for my sins, I have nothing. I am void of life. He is everything good I have. He is the one who keeps the record of my life. I report to my God alone. "Help me to be holy because you are a holy God."

Chapter 18
YOU ARE MY REST.

Matthew11:28-30

"Come to me, all you who are tired from carrying heavy loads, and I will give you rest. Take my yoke and put it on you, and learn from me, because I am gentle and humble in spirit; and you will find rest. For the yoke I will give you is easy, and the load I will put on you is light. ``

Psalm 91:1-3

Whoever goes to the Lord for safety, whoever remains under the protection of the Almighty can say to him, "You are my defender and protector. You are my God; in you I trust." He will keep you safe from all hidden dangers and from all deadly diseases.

Psalm 91:4

He will cover you with his wings; you will be safe in his care; his faithfulness will protect and defend you.

Isaiah 9:2-3

The people who walked in darkness have seen a great light. They lived in a land of shadows, but now light is shinning on them. You have given them great joy, LORD; you have made them happy. They rejoice in what you have done, as people rejoice when they harvest their corn or when they divide captured wealth. For you have broken the yoke that burdened them and the rod that beat their shoulders.

Zechariah 10:12

"I will make my people strong; they will worship and obey me." The LORD has spoken.

- ❖ You do not deserve this weakness, you do not deserve to be sick, and you have done nothing wrong, God will take away this victimisation and heal you and make you strong again. When you are strong praise him for giving you the right to overcome through Jesus Christ. His saving power brings healing to you his child.

Romans 8:33-34

Who will accuse God`s chosen people? God himself declared them not guilty! Who then, will condemn them? Not Christ Jesus, who died, or rather, who was raised to life and is at the right- hand side of God, pleading with him for us!

Psalm 103:1-5

Praise the LORD, my soul! All my being, praise his holy name! Praise the Lord, my soul, and do not forget how kind he is. He forgives all my sins and heals all my diseases. He keeps me from the grave and blesses me with love and mercy. He fills my life with good things, so that I stay young and strong like an eagle.

Chapter 19

YOUR EYES GOD.

Hebrews 4:12-13

For the word of God is living and active. Sharper than any double- edged sword, it penetrates even to dividing soul and spirit, joints and marrow; It judges the thoughts and attitudes of the heart. Nothing in all creation is hidden from God`s sight. Everything is uncovered and laid bare before the eyes of him to whom we must give account.

Psalm 10:14

But you do see; you take notice of trouble and suffering and are always ready to help.

Psalm17:8-9

Protect me as would your very eyes; hide me in the shadow of your wings, from the attack of the wicked.

Psalm 121:4-5

The protector of Israel never dozes or sleeps. The LORD will guard you; he is by your side to protect you.

Psalm 139:3-6

You see me; whether I am working or resting; you know all my actions. Even before I speak, you already know what I will say. You are all around me on every side; you protect me with your power. Your knowledge of me is too deep; it is beyond my understand

Psalm 139:8-12.

If I went up to heaven, you will be there; If I lay down in the world of the dead, you would be there. If I flew away beyond the east or lived in the farthest place in the west, you will be there to lead me; you would be there to help me. I could ask the darkness to hide me or the light round me to turn into night, but even darkness is not dark for you, and the night is as bright as the day. Darkness and light are the same to you.

Psalm 139:15-16

When my bones were being formed, carefully put together in my mother`s womb, when I was growing there in secret, You knew that I was there- you saw me before I was born. The days allotted to me had all been recorded in your book, before any of them ever begun.

Chapter 20
HIDE ME, FAITHFUL GOD

Psalm3:3

But you, O LORD, are always my shield from danger; you give me victory and restore my courage.

Psalm 8:1-2

O LORD, our Lord, your greatness is seen in all the world! Your praises reaches up to the heavens; it is sung by children and babies. You are safe and secure from all your enemies; you stop anyone who opposes you.

Hebrews 2:14-15

Since the children, as he calls them, are people of flesh and blood, Jesus himself became like them and shared their human nature. He did this so that through his death he might destroy the Devil, who have the power over death, and in this way set free those who were slaves all their lives because of the fear of death.

2Thesalonnians3:3

But the Lord is faithful, and he will strengthen and protect you from the evil one.

Isaiah 54:17

No weapon forged against you will prevail, and you will refute every tongue that accuses you.

Psalm12:5

"But now I will come," says the LORD, "because the needy are oppressed and the persecuted groan in pain. I will give them the security they long for."

Psalm13:3

Look at me, O LORD my God, and answer me. Restore my strength; don`t let me die.

❖ You will see God`s face when you are declared healed! No more tears, no more fear, no more pain and you will forever depend and trust upon him. His healing power brings assurance of his greatness. You will live a confident life full of his light and knowledge of his presence. God is forever protecting you, all you need is to trust and believe in the one he sent as our helper and saviour, Jesus Christ.

Psalm 16: 2

I say to the LORD, "You are my Lord; all the good things I have come from you."

Psalm 32:7

You are my hiding place; you will protect me from trouble and surround me with songs of deliverance.

Psalm 33:4

For the word of the Lord is right and true; he is faithful in all he does.

Psalm118:13-14

I was fiercely attacked and was being defeated, but the LORD helped me. The LORD makes me powerful and strong; he has saved me.

Chapter 21

HOPE FOR THE HOPELESS.

2 Corinthians 4:8

We are hard pressed on every side, but not crushed; perplexed, but not in despair; persecuted, but not abandoned; struck down but not destroyed.

Isaiah 52:10

The LORD will use his power; he will save his people, and the world will see it.

Revelation 5:9

"You are worthy to take the scroll and to break open its seals. For you were killed, and by your death you bought for God people from every tribe, language, nation, and race."

- ❖ Jesus died for all of us. The Holy Spirit brings us together as one. We are all children of a great God through Jesus who died for us on the cross for us to be forgiven. He brought love and unity to the world. The devil stands accused and defeated.

Psalm 29:10-11

The LORD rules over the deep waters; He rules as king forever. The LORD gives strength to his people and he blesses them with peace.

- ❖ No matter how deep or wide your trouble is, God is able to help you because of his mighty, supernatural and triumphant power. He created all things, small and grand and nothing escapes his hand, he is able to save in his sovereignty and because he loves us and is merciful, by his grace we are healed.

1Peter 5:10-11

But after you have suffered for a little while, the God of all grace, who calls to share his eternal glory in union with Christ, will himself perfect you and give you firmness, strength, and a sure foundation. To him be the power forever!

Chapter 22

RE-BIRTH.

Isaiah 62:2-5

You will be called by a new name, a name given by the LORD himself. You will be like a beautiful crown for the LORD. No longer will you be called "Forsaken," or your land be called "Deserted Wife." Your new name will be "God is pleased with her." Your land will be called "Happily Married," Because the LORD is pleased with you and will be like a husband to your land. Like a young man taking a virgin as a bride, He who formed you will marry you. As a groom is delighted with his bride, So your God will delight in you.

Galatians 4:4-6

But when the right time finally came, God sent his own Son. He came as the Son of a human mother and lived under the Jewish Law, to redeem those who were under the Law, so that we might become God`s sons. To show that you are his sons, God sent the Spirit of his Son into our hearts, the Spirit who cries out, "Father, my Father."

2Corinthians 3:17-18

Now the, "the Lord" in this passage is the Spirit; and where the Spirit of the lord is present, there is freedom. All of us, then, reflect the glory of the Lord with uncovered faces; and that same glory, coming from the Lord, who is the Spirit, transforms us into his likeness in an ever greater degree of glory.

Romans 8:5-6

Those who live as their human nature tells them to, have their minds controlled by what human nature wants. Those who live as the Spirit tells them to, have their minds controlled by what the Spirit wants. To be controlled by human nature results in death; to be controlled by the Spirit result in life and peace.

1John 5:11-12

The testimony is this: God has given us eternal life, and this life has its source in his Son. Whoever has the Son has this life; whoever does not have the Son of God does not have life.

BIBLIOGRAPHY

1. *Finger of God.*
2. *Good News Bible, Today`s English Version. 1976*

CPSIA information can be obtained at www.ICGtesting.com
Printed in the USA
LVOW111013141012

302782LV00003B/169/P